The Big 5-0

THE BIG 5 TURNS 50

Credits

Philadelphia Daily News

Michael Days, Editor
Pat McLoone, Executive Sports Editor
Josh Barnett, Sports Editor

Book Editors

Jim DeStefano
Paul Vigna
Bob Vetrone Jr.

Designed by: Jon Snyder

PHOTO CREDITS

Cover Photos: Main: Rick Bowmer (Palestra). Bottom (from left): Yong Kim (Donnie Carr, Tim Begley); George Reynolds (Jameer Nelson); Yong Kim (Pepe Sanchez, Curtis Sumpter).

Joey Adams: Page 26
Alejandro A. Alvarez: Pages 64-67
Rick Bowmer: Page 6, 21
Prentice Cole: Page 15 (right), 34, 86, 89
Yong Kim: Page 31 (right), 41 (top), 43, 53
Bob Laramie: Page 14 (right), 45, 54 (top), 71
Norman Lono: Page 37
G.W. Miller III: Page 25, 28 (right)
Sam Psoras: Page 36, 41 (bottom), 78 (right)
George Reynolds: Page 8 (top left), 12 (left), 13 (left), 47, 52 (left), 88
Elwood P. Smith: Page 31 (left), 33, 49 (right), 62-63, 82 (bottom)

Temple Urban Archives: Page 22 (right)

Courtesy of La Salle: Page 18-19
Courtesy of Penn: Page 10, 73 (left), 76 (right)
Courtesy of Saint Joseph's: Page 16 (left), 38, 39, 40 (left), 70, 72, 75 (top)
Courtesy of Temple: Page 46 (left), 49 (left), 73 (right)
Courtesy of Villanova: Page 74

All others are Daily News/Inquirer File Photos

For additional copies:
Visit **www.philly.com/store** to order additional copies of this and other books published by Philadelphia Newspapers, Inc.

ISBN 1-58822-051-6

Table of Contents

DEDICATION

We all should be so fortunate as to have just one job doing something we love. My father had many. Since its inception a half-century ago to his passing last March, Bob Vetrone Sr. served at the Big 5's beck and call on many levels. And for that, this book has been respectfully dedicated to him.

From the very public stages provided by TV cameras and radio microphones to the mundane solitude of copying and filing, he tackled each and every task with a sense of purpose, with a sense of pride, with a sense of humor.

He performed many duties over the years for an institution he held as close to his heart as any. He wrote it; he broadcast it; he telecast it; he administered it. But most of all, he enjoyed it.

For him, it was never about the wins and losses; there was always another game, another season, another freshman class. More than that, it was about the people — the bench warmers and the starters, the vendors and the ticket takers, the fans in the front row and those pressed into the corners…

So to all who have helped form a unique and satisfying sporting experience over the years, please consider this a salute directly from him:

Job well done.

— *Bob Vetrone Jr.*

Joined at the hoop

UNLIKELY UNION OF FIVE
SCHOOLS A SOURCE OF
PHILLY PRIDE

By
Rich Hofmann

It began, lo these many years ago, as a loveless marriage. Villanova and La Salle had not played a basketball game against each other in 20 years, and Villanova and Penn had not played in more than 30 years, and this school wasn't talking to that school, and everybody walked to the altar while trying to figure out exactly what angle the other guys were working. And so Philadelphia's Big 5 began, out of a desire that was neither pure nor innocent. They were just trying to make a buck.

Fifty years later, the wrinkles show. They are like an old couple sometimes. They bicker, and they hold ancient grudges, and they deliver slights they don't even realize they are delivering at times after decades of familiarity, of taking each other for granted. They also laugh at private jokes that only they find funny, and fondly recall shared memories, and finish each other's sentences. No one can imagine them apart.

La Salle. Pennsylvania. Saint Joseph's. Temple. Villanova. Their union is a civic treasure and a national oddity.

People in other cities couldn't believe it when it happened. People in other cities can't believe it today. They are five schools with five different academic missions. They play in three different leagues. They compete for some of the same players. They fight over every bit of the same spotlight. Yet they come together, 10 times a year, in the interest of raising fratricide to glory.

La Salle. Pennsylvania. Saint Joseph's. Temple. Villanova. It all makes perfect sense, somehow.

Matrimony, fratricide — the metaphors are as mixed as the memories, most of them cast in the heat of the Palestra. You cannot tell the story of the Big 5 without acknowledging the importance of the arena on 33rd Street. Only about half of the Big 5 games are played there now, and nobody on any of the current teams knows much of the lore. It wasn't always sold out, either, not even in the good, old

The storied Palestra on Penn's campus is as much a part of Big 5 lore as great games and dynamic players.

Palestra official scorer Bob McKee (left) received Big 5 Hall of Fame plaque from Paul Rubincam in 1990.

PA announcer John McAdams called the Palestra 'college basketball's most historic gym.'

days. You can check some 1970s box scores and notice that the announced attendance of many doubleheaders bore a striking resemblance to the half-time score of the second game; 49-41, 4,941. No matter. The people and the place remain intertwined.

The Palestra. It is the place where Bob McKee, the official scorer, wore a red cap so players could find him and check in amid the chaos of the sidelines. Where a semi-street person named Yo Yo would toddle out and shoot an underhanded free throw, and that would suffice many nights as the halftime entertainment. Where John McAdams would begin his public-address announcements by declaring your presence in "college basketball's most historic gym," and where Dan Baker and Bob Vetrone would do the radio broadcasts amid the din, and where Al Meltzer or Les Keiter would climb into the tiny crow's nest of a television booth above the

The Big 5 mascots (from left), circa 1970: the Wildcat, Hawk, Quaker, Explorer and Owl.

Temple's Tim Perry, Villanova's Harold Pressley eye shot during game in 1984.

The day five became one

By
Bob Vetrone Jr.

For an institution that has given us: (a) what might have been the greatest upset in college basketball championship history; (b) a non-scholarship school reaching the Final Four; and (c) a game delayed by a bomb threat — its biggest surprise may have been its first.

On Nov. 23, 1954, University of Pennsylvania president Dr. Gaylord P. Harnwell stunned the local and national sporting world by announcing that Philadelphia's five major college basketball teams would, beginning in 1955-56, combine to play 30 doubleheaders at the Palestra in an unprecedented cooperative agreement.

Among the games would be a full 10-game round-robin schedule among all five schools, from which a City Series champion would be crowned.

Villanova, which had met Penn just once (1922), had been playing a majority of its home games at the Palestra for a half-dozen years. But La Salle, Saint Joseph's and Temple were putting on doubleheaders of their own down the street at Convention Hall.

Also unprecedented was the financial consideration. According to the statement, "the five participating institutions will share equally in the season's net proceeds from the games."

The new arrangement — "which almost certainly will be called the Big Five," according to the next day's *Inquirer* — required improvements to the Palestra, nearly 30 years old at that point.

It was expected to seat 8,000 for the first season, "with the possibility of an increase to 10,000 after the first year if interest warrants," according to Harnwell's statement.

"Press, radio and TV facilities will be improved since it is anticipated that the Palestra will become the center of intercollegiate basketball in the East...[The Big 5 arrangement] will be followed, I hope, by others of mutual benefit to all involved."

On Saturday, Dec. 3, 1955, La Salle played Muhlenberg, Saint Joseph's took on Rhode Island and the Philadelphia face of college basketball changed forever.

The City Series itself was christened 11 days later, when Saint Joseph's and Villanova met after La Salle's victory over Lafayette.

"It's bound to increase interest," said Villanova coach Al Severance at the luncheon that bore the Big 5, "and will eventually make Philadelphia the basketball capital of the nation."

Captain JIM SMITH
Villanova University

Captain MIKE FALLON
St. Joseph's College

THE INQUIRER TROPHY
For City Series Winner

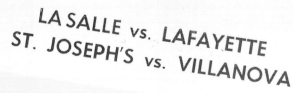

LA SALLE vs. LAFAYETTE
ST. JOSEPH'S vs. VILLANOVA

Palestra Illustrated

DECEMBER 14, 1955

PRICE 25c

Palestra staples (from left) Yo Yo, and radio broadcasters Bob Vetrone and Dan Baker.

south stands and bring the magic into your home. Except that it wasn't the same. You really did have to be there.

To sit along press row is to witness a spectacle that assaults your senses — torturing your ears with the noise of the place, and sweat-soaking your shirt with the midwinter heat. Sitting there in that first row, the visiting coach stalking in front of you, you become his foil sometimes ("Can you believe that call?") and often can eavesdrop on his huddle. It is a seat like no other.

But wherever the games are played, and whoever is playing them, there is a shared style of play. You hear the words "typical Big 5 game," and your first thought is a close game. But that isn't it, not exactly. A typical Big 5 game is rugged, first and always — and it is officiated that way, as if the referees understand that history demands that they back off. A typical Big 5 game is more about endurance than art, which is the natural result of that physical style. A typical Big 5 game is a grudge fight, even if the players themselves hold none of the grudges — because there are thousands of sixth men in the stands, and they know where all of the bodies are buried, and they are an integral part of this process.

Because that is what the Big 5, and that is what these 50 years, have been about. This association of five schools and their basketball programs has not made any of them rich. What it has done is make them a vibrant part of this community — a source of pride and a rallying point for their alumni; a spectacle unlike any other in their sport, where five schools play each other every year simply because it is the right thing to do.

The memories of games and players blur over time, but there are some things you never forget — how refreshing the cold feels as you leave the Palestra on a February night, and how your ears ring for blocks as you walk to your car.

That much has not changed. Fifty years later, the Big 5 still grabs your senses and won't let go.

Sweet 13

OUR ALL-TIME BIG 5 TEAM WOULD DOMINATE ANY ERA

By
Dick Jerardi

How do you define greatness, exactly? It is probably not unlike former Supreme Court Justice Potter Stewart's description of pornography: "I know it when I see it."

Approximately 2,000 players have suited up for Big 5 games in its 50-year history. There have been more than a few great players and great performances. And we know them when we see them.

When the Big 5 and the *Daily News* combined to select an all-time Big 5 team on the 40th anniversary in 1995, we came up with 10 players. Ten years later, room must be made for three more.

Today, Division I teams are allowed 13 scholarship players. So, in honor of the modern game and with reverence to a 50-year tradition, here is a team of 13 great Big 5 players that has two of everything and a few reinforcements after that.

The point guards are Temple's Guy Rodgers and Saint Joseph's Jameer Nelson.

Rodgers was there at the start of the Big 5, the first

Jameer Nelson (left) sparked comparisons to a point guard of another era, Guy Rodgers (above, shooting).

DICK JERARDI'S ALL-TIME TEAM

POINT GUARDS
Guy Rodgers, Temple
Jameer Nelson, Saint Joseph's

SHOOTING GUARDS
Mark Macon, Temple
Kerry Kittles, Villanova

SMALL FORWARDS
Kenny Durrett, La Salle
Lionel Simmons, La Salle

POWER FORWARDS
Howard Porter, Villanova
Michael Brooks, La Salle

CENTERS
Ed Pinckney, Villanova
Cliff Anderson, Saint Joseph's

SWINGMEN/SUBS
Wali Jones, Villanova
Larry Cannon, La Salle
Corky Calhoun, Penn

great player. In 3 years at Temple, Rodgers twice got the Owls to the Final Four, a place the school has not been since. He scored 1,767 points, still fifth all-time at Temple. Sadly, they did not keep assist totals back then. Rodgers was a one-man fastbreak who saw everything and everyone. He was in fast motion, but, to him, the game was in slow motion. He ran with Hal Lear and Bill "Pickles" Kennedy. He won big with both of them. In his three seasons, Temple was 74-16. Some think the term point guard was invented for the Philly guard. If that was so, Rodgers was the model.

Nelson holds his school's record for points, assists, steals and wins in a 4-year period. He was the national player of the year in 2003-04. He took a team that had won 36 times in three seasons before he arrived to a team that won 30 games in the season before he left. The true believers never compared another Big 5 point guard to Rodgers — until Nelson. He could play fast, slow or in-between. He sensed the rhythm of a game before games even had any rhythm. He instinctively always seemed to

y Kittles scored
3 points, first on
anova's career list.

Mark Macon, a perfect fit for John Chaney's system, was a starter at Temple in all four of his seasons.

Two talented small forwards from La Salle were Kenny Durrett (left) and Lionel Simmons.

Ed Pinckney (above) and Michael Brooks could defend as well as score.

know the right thing to do and when to do it.

Rodgers died in 2001, near the end of Nelson's first season at St. Joe's. Great point guards always have an impeccable sense of timing. Somehow, Rodgers must have known his replacement finally had arrived.

The shooting guards are Temple's Mark Macon and Villanova's Kerry Kittles.

Macon (2,609 points) is Temple's all-time leading scorer. More than any other player, he epitomizes the John Chaney era at Temple. Fearless and incredibly athletic, Macon was Chaney. He understood his unique coach and would do anything to make him proud. As a freshman, Macon was the signature player on the first Big 5 team to be ranked No. 1. As

a senior, he had a final shot in the air that would have tied North Carolina at the buzzer of their Elite Eight NCAA game.

Kittles (2,243 points) is the leading scorer at Villanova, the proud home of six 2,000-point scorers. He is also first in steals and 10th in assists. The best player on Villanova's only Big East champion, Kittles was a great passing-lane defender with speed and quickness that were almost beyond belief

The small forwards are La Salle's Kenny Durrett and Lionel Simmons.

Durrett was going to be an NBA All-Star, probably a Hall of Famer. He had guard skills in a big man's body. There was simply nothing he could not do on a basketball court. If he had played around the turn of the century instead of three decades earlier, when college basketball was just a regional game, he would have been all over the Internet, on the covers of magazines and the subject of daily cable TV discussions.

When he was in town for the 40th anniversary celebration, Durrett, seated one afternoon in the same Palestra he had lit up like nobody else, said: "I was just sitting here now reminiscing, just hearing the sounds again and just being in here. This is a very special place for me. There is just something about this building that is magical."

And there was something magical about Durrett. He blew out a knee in his senior year so he never really had a chance to prove in the NBA what everybody in Philly already knew. He was one of the ones. A few years after he was honored, Durrett died, far too young. What he did in the Big 5 never will die. When they are naming the 100th anniversary Big 5 team, Kenny Durrett will be a lock.

Simmons was more of a power forward in college, but he played like a small forward. He had a wonderful understanding of basketball's geometry, which was why he was such a great passer and shot-blocker. He knew time and place. He knew how to play. Game after game, he was always there, his numbers mind-numbingly consistent. His 28.4-point average in 1988-89 is No. 1 in Big 5 history. He is one of just six Division I players to score 3,000 points. His 3,217 points are third all-time. When he finally was done, his team had won 100 games in four seasons. He was the national player of the year

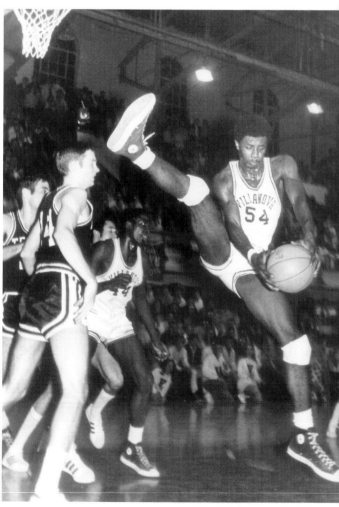

Howard Porter averaged 14.8 rebounds a game during his career.

Despite being only 6-4, Cliff Anderson played center and averaged 14.6 rebounds during his career.

in 1989-90.

The power forwards are Villanova's Howard Porter and La Salle's Michael Brooks.

Porter and Durrett had the Big 5's greatest individual rivalry. Porter's size and athleticism are probably unmatched in Big 5 history. There was just nobody like him. He averaged 22.8 points and 14.8 rebounds for his career. His 2,026 points are fifth all-time at Villanova. His 1,317 rebounds are No. 1. During UCLA's run of seven consecutive national championships, it was Porter and Villanova that gave the Bruins their toughest championship game (1971).

Brooks was a scoring machine. His 2,628 points would be best at almost every school in America. He could play inside, outside or in between. He was

Wali Jones was smart, skillful and tough.

somehow graceful and powerful. He was going to be the captain of the 1980 United States team that never played an Olympic game because of the Moscow boycott.

The centers are Villanova's Ed Pinckney and Saint Joseph's Cliff Anderson.

Pinckney was the best player on the only Big 5-era team to win a national championship. He was voted the Most Outstanding Player of the 1985 Final Four when Villanova played its perfect game and upset Georgetown for the championship. And it wasn't like he got hot for a weekend. He is seventh all-time at Villanova in scoring (1,865 points), third in blocks (253) and fourth in rebounds (1,107). The Big 5 has been noted for many things, but never its great centers. Pinckney was a great center.

Anderson was a 6-4 center. He really was. He was on the receiving end of lobs from 6-6 point guard Matt Guokas Jr. Anderson averaged 20.6 points and an incredible 14.6 rebounds in his 84-game career. He is the fifth all-time leading scorer (1,728 points) at St. Joe's and first in rebounds (1,228). He averaged 26.5 points during his senior season when he was the last star left from some superior St. Joe's

teams.

The swingmen/super subs are Villanova's Wali Jones, La Salle's Larry Cannon and Penn's Corky Calhoun.

Jones helped swing the early Big 5 dominance of St. Joe's back toward Villanova with his high basketball IQ, toughness and skill. Cannon modeled his courtlong charges after Rodgers, his idol. Calhoun was a forward his first two seasons before moving to the backcourt when Steve Bilsky and Dave Wohl graduated. All you need to know about Calhoun is that his three Penn teams were 78-6, 41-1 in the Ivy League.

When the 40th anniversary team was honored at halftime of a Penn-Temple game on Feb. 14, 1995, Cannon lingered longest after the game.

"It's just hard to describe," he said that night. "I'm a Philadelphian. I grew up with this from the time I saw the first game at the Palestra. The only thing I would trade this for would be a chance to be a sophomore at La Salle again and back out here playing. Or it could be that we were all seniors and there was 10 of us and we could just throw it up and run up and down."

Larry Cannon cut down the nets when La Salle defeated Villanova during its 23-1 season in 1968-69.

Corky Calhoun was versatile enough to play both forward and guard.

The stuff of legend

BIG 5 HAS HISTORY OF OUTSTANDING COACHES

By Rich Hofmann

You could just list them, of course. There are only 34 of them in the whole first half-century of the Big 5. You could read them off, one after another, and realize what you always knew: While the players of the Big 5 were good, the coaches might have been better.

What else is there to say, really? Philadelphia-as-a-basketball-town always has been about instruction, at least on some level. More kids get more good coaching at an earlier age in Philadelphia than just about anywhere, and they always have — and if that is a parochial prejudice, unproved and unprovable,

so be it.

But it is a mind-set, and it is an ethic, and it has risen through the levels over the years — with the Big 5 schools at the top. It is just good basketball, and it always has been, and you never will be able to discount the role of the men in charge.

Rollie Massimino exhorted. John Chaney scowled. And Paul Westhead dreamed of offensive innovations during the game and quoted Shakespeare after.

Jack Ramsay studied from his perch, on one knee. Speedy Morris studied, too, but with arms folded in front of him. And then there was Jimmy Lynam, who danced and leaped and hugged his daughter, Dei.

They were all different. They were mostly excellent. Massimino might just have been the best of them all, a statement that will pain people who never can forget Villanova's decision (along with Temple) to temporarily alter the Big 5's round-robin schedule in the late 1980s. But Rollie was a master of his day — before the shot clock, before the three-point line. He will forever be summed up by three words that he tended to shout near the end of close games, after he had done the calculations in his head — time, score, situation — and determined that his team couldn't lose.

Three words: "We've got enough!"

You wonder if he yelled them on April 1, 1985, in Lexington, Ky., when Villanova won the title.

Massimino had come to Villanova from Penn, where he had been an assistant coach. That was not uncommon, back in the day — Westhead, for instance, was a St. Joe's graduate who ended up coaching at La Salle in the '70s. It is less imaginable now, though. In 2005, only Penn's Fran Dunphy, who played and coached at La Salle, is a crossover. As for the rest, in many cases it almost seems an impossibility — a St. Joe's coach going to Villanova, for instance, or a Temple coach going to St. Joe's.

If the coaches today are not as close as they once

Neither Temple's Harry Litwack (left) nor Villanova's Jack Kraft needed smoke and mirrors to be successful.

Rollie Massimino got a lift from his players after Villanova won the national championship in 1985.

Speedy Morris was known to show his emotions during his tenure at La Salle.

St. Joe's Jack Ramsay often coached while perched on one knee.

were — and they aren't — they are still closer than anyone has a right to expect. They do charity work together for "Coaches vs. Cancer." They share information at times. And even amid the scrapes — with Chaney in the middle of most of them these days — there always seems to be a peacemaker. Today it is Dunphy. Fifteen years ago, it was Dan Baker, the Big 5's executive director. Thirty years ago, it was Temple coach Don Casey. They were people who took the Big 5's legacy seriously, who guarded it as a public trust. They always seemed ready to keep those lines between schools crossing and intersect-

ing in such a Philadelphia way.

Like on April 1, 1985, in Lexington, Ky., when Harry Booth — the former St. Joe's coach — sat on Massimino's bench as an assistant coach.

Booth was one in a long line of St. Joe's grads who ended up coaching the Hawks — Widener's Phil Martelli, ironically, broke the mold and has enjoyed the school's greatest modern success. But that was the St. Joe's way, to keep it in the family (and, for the record, Martelli enjoyed honorary citizenship on Hawk Hill after a decade as an assistant coach).

John Chaney has guided Temple's fortunes since 1982, rarely with a dull moment.

Jim Lynam (top) is one of a
number of St. Joe's graduates
to have coached the Hawks.
Current coach Phil Martelli
graduated from Widener.

involved as the Big 5 blossomed. And so, St. Joe's coaches had to live up to Ramsay and Lynam, and Chaney had a new building to fill with an old style of play, and La Salle struggled with its identity, and Penn tried (and succeeded) in competing without scholarships, and Villanova coaches always have been chasing that magical night in Rupp Arena — chasing and falling short.

And on April 1, 1985, in Lexington, Ky., one of the people who chased that dream for years was also on Massimino's bench — Steve Lappas, then a kid assistant coach.

Lappas is one of the good guys who couldn't get over all of the hurdles. There have been others. Because coaching in the Big 5 is hard. The competition is relentless, and the programs are clean, and the shortcuts are not obvious. So much has changed for these men over the decades.

Back when this all began, basketball conferences around here were unimportant, really — not the structures that ruled a coach's life. Back in the beginning, postseason tournaments were rewards for excellence and opportunities for greatness — not measuring sticks used by alumni to beat

Paul Westhead, a St. Joe's grad, coached La Salle for most of the 1970s.

Each school followed a pattern. La Salle tended to stay with local guys, until recently — and even John Giannini had his time at Rowan. Penn had more of a mixture, but still leaned to locals and legacies. Temple's 50 years has been bracketed by two legends — Harry Litwack at the beginning, and Chaney at the end. Villanova has looked around a little more.

They all have faced pressures unique to their schools — not so much at the beginning, but in later years. Because the business got bigger, and the money at stake more important, and the fans more

coaches over the head. It is so different now. A Big 5 coach's life is very complicated. There are many masters and few easy wins.

It really was simpler in the beginning. Back then, there were these five men: Litwack at Temple, Ramsay at St. Joe's, Ray Stanley at Penn, Jim Pollard at La Salle and Al Severance at Villanova. That is where it started.

And on April 1, 1985, in Lexington, Ky., Severance died in a hotel room on the morning of Villanova basketball's greatest day. And the lines continued to intersect.

Penn coach Fran
Dunphy, who played at
La Salle, is the Big 5's
modern peacemaker.

Exploring excellence

DURRETT, GOLA FUELED LA SALLE'S 23-1 POWERHOUSE

By
Bob Cooney

O f all the debates through the years concerning teams, players and coaches that have graced and paced Big 5 basketball, few end in agreement.

Two usually do.

That Ken Durrett was the best player in the Big 5 since its inception in 1955.

And that the La Salle team of 1968-69 — on which Durrett, a forward, starred as a sophomore — was the best in Big 5 history.

Although the program has fallen on hard times in recent years, it is impossible to deny the rich history of basketball at 20th and Olney.

The 1968-69 team was coached by La Salle great Tom Gola. Considered by many the greatest college player in the city's history, Gola was coaching at the school he had led to the NCAA championship as a junior 15 years earlier.

In that marvelous five-game tournament run in 1954, Gola averaged 22.8 points and 20.4 rebounds and earned the tournament's outstanding player award. After the season, he was named the national player of the year.

Gola finished his career with 2,461 points and 2,201 rebounds, still an NCAA record.

It was only fitting that the school's greatest play-

First-year coach Tom Gola got his point across in 1968-69 as La Salle finished 23-1. Listening to this blackboard session were (from left) Fran Dunphy, Roland Taylor, Ed Szczesny and Ken Durrett.

There was quite a celebration when Lionel Simmons scored his 3,000th point.

er coach the best team since he graduated. There was one problem, however. The 23-1 Explorers reached a No. 2 national ranking but were on probation stemming from NCAA violations during the regime of previous coach Jim Harding. They were unable to compete in the NCAA Tournament.

But oh, how good they were. In his first year as a college player (freshmen were ineligible for the varsity), all Durrett did was average 20 points and close to 12 rebounds. At 6-8, he was blessed with a power forward's body and ballhandling skills that were rare for a player his size.

"He was skinny-strong," described former Durrett teammate Jim Crawford, a Big 5 Hall of Famer. "His skills were ahead of his time in that he could score from the outside and he could handle

and pass the ball so well. Also, if a player or a team tried to stop him one way, Kenny was smart enough to figure out a way to beat their game plan. He had it all."

Durrett's game was perfectly suited for the fast-break style that Gola implemented in his first season as coach.

"Coach Gola was a perfect fit for our team," said Fran Dunphy, a reserve on that team and longtime coach at Penn. "Coach Harding was a real disciplinarian, with his 3-hour practices. That turned out to be very beneficial for us, though. When coach Gola came and let us loose, all the parts fell into place."

Durrett had the perfect complement in senior forward Larry Cannon. The sturdily built, 6-4 Cannon was already a proven scorer (19-point career aver-

Michael Brooks (left) and Donnie Carr each scored more than 2,000 career points.

age), but was able to fashion his game around the wonderfully talented Durrett. Already a great all-around player, Cannon's overall game shined even more after the arrival of Durrett.

"Larry was extraordinary physically without lifting a weight," Dunphy said. "There wasn't an ounce of fat on him. He was a great passer and a great scorer, although he didn't need to be as much with Kenny. He was a great competitor who loved the game."

The backcourt of Roland "Fatty" Taylor, a terrific point guard with a tenacity for defense and a wonderful gift for decision-making, and shooter Bernie Williams ("the net hardly ever moved when he shot," Dunphy said), was ideal for Gola's style.

The final piece of the puzzle was Stan Wlodarczyk.

"He was like [former Sixers forward] Bobby Jones before Bobby Jones," Dunphy said. "He could shut people down defensively and was always in the right spot on the court.

"It was a solid group all the way around. We had the foundation of the discipline from coach Harding, and then coach Gola just let us play. It worked out just about perfect."

"Just about," in that the Explorers finished the season with a romp over West Chester in tiny Hollinger Field House, instead of on the national stage — maybe facing powerful UCLA and center Lew Alcindor.

We'll never know.

A game that many refer to when speaking of Durrett was a 91-76 victory over 7-foot All-American Jim McDaniels and Western Kentucky at the Palestra on Jan. 16, 1971, when Durrett went off for 45 points.

"They had four great athletes and a 7-footer," Crawford said. "They pressed all over. All we did was throw over the press and let Kenny go one-on-one with the 7-footer. It was no contest."

In his three seasons at La Salle, Durrett was a three-time Big 5 MVP and a consensus All-American in 1971. He was averaging 27 points and 12 rebounds his senior season under coach Paul Westhead when he was felled by a torn ACL late in the season. What seemed like a sure successful NBA career never materialized, and his playing days were over after four unproductive seasons as a pro.

Sadly, Durrett's life ended too soon; he died of a heart attack in 2001 at the age of 52.

Durrett leads a list of many great forwards to wear an Explorers uniform. Lionel Simmons was named the 1990 national player of the year after averaging 26.5 points and 11.1 rebounds. During his four seasons, Simmons scored 3,217 points

Tom Gola led La Salle to the national championship in 1954 and came back to coach the 23-1 team in 1968-69.

Fran Dunphy, the longtime coach at Penn, played three seasons at La Salle.

Ken Durrett suffered a serious knee injury as a senior that hindered his pro career.

Rasual Butler scored 2,125 points during his 4-year career.

(third in Division I history), grabbed 1,429 rebounds and participated in 100 victories. His arrival from Southern High School coincided with that of coach Bill "Speedy" Morris, who spent 15 seasons at La Salle and won a school-record 238 games.

Thirty of those victories came in Simmons' senior season, when the Explorers went 30-2 and had a 22-game winning streak that included their first NCAA Tournament win since 1983.

Perhaps the highlight of the season occurred on Feb. 22 at the Civic Center. That was the night the classy Simmons, a 6-7 forward with the silky-smooth game, canned a free throw midway through the first half in a romp over Manhattan for point No. 3,000. It set off a wild celebration among the 8,136 fans, and firmly planted him as one of college basketball's all-time greats.

"Years from now," Morris after the game, "we're all, including the coaches, going to be able to say we played with one of the greatest players in the history of the game."

The years have passed. Those sentiments haven't.

Simmons would close out his dominating career with a second-round loss to Clemson in the NCAA Tournament. He was chosen eighth overall by the Sacramento Kings a few months later and had a productive, 7-year NBA career.

Joining Gola and Simmons as national players of the year was slick forward Michael Brooks. A prolific scorer (2,628 career points) with deadly midrange scoring ability and a rugged inside game, Brooks captured the honor after the 1979-80 season in which he led the club to a 22-9 record under coach Dave "Lefty" Ervin, averaging 24.1 points and 11.5 boards.

Three other Explorers have cracked the 2,000-point barrier. Rasual Butler (1998-2002) is fourth on the school's list with 2,125 points. Donnie Carr (1996-2000) scored 2,067 and Steve Black (1981-85) had 2,012.

Current forward Steve Smith, who was named the Atlantic 10's co-player of the year in 2004-05, could join those elite names; he enters his final season with 1,389 points.

Some other prolific La Salle scorers were guard Hubie Marshall (21.3-point career average) and forward Frank Corace (19.3) in the 1960s; forwards Joe Bryant (20.7) and Bill Taylor (19.0) in the 1970s; and guards Kareem Townes (23.8) and Randy Woods (20.6) in the 1990s.

Through the years, skillful players have given La Salle fans reason for optimism, but there hasn't been much of that at 20th and Olney for a long time. Twelve consecutive losing seasons and rape allegations in 2004 against three former players that led to the resignation of coach Billy Hahn brought a once-proud program to its lowest level.

The hiring of John Giannini, a respected coach and recruiter, has elevated hopes again. Hopes of years gone past. Hopes of glory days.

Turning points

BILSKY'S LATE FIELD GOAL IN 1969 CLASSIC SANK 'NOVA, ELEVATED QUAKERS

By
Kevin Mulligan

Jerome Allen...John Beecroft...Tim Begley...Bob Bigelow...Steve Bilsky...Corky Calhoun...Dick Censits...Chuck Daly...Fran Dunphy...

Sixteen years had passed since Ernie Beck's unequaled 1950-53 greatness predated the Big 5. Six seasons had come and gone since a 1962-63 University of Pennsylvania team, led by Rhodes scholar John Wideman, posted the school's first winning record (3-1) against city opponents and finished tied for first in the Big 5.

But a 5-19 record by Penn against Big 5 rivals La Salle, Saint Joseph's, Temple and Villanova closed out the '60s. Only once during that span, in 1965-66, behind Jeff Neuman and Stan Pawlak — who in '66

Bobby Willis cut down a souvenir when Penn defeated St. John's and advanced to the 1979 Final Four in Salt Lake City.

Steve Bilsky's game-winning shot against Villanova in 1969 was a defining moment in Penn's program.

led Penn to its first Ivy League championship — did the Quakers win more than one City Series game (2-2).

In 11 of the first 14 years of the Big 5, born in a meeting of athletic directors at Penn in November 1954, Penn did not win more than one Big 5 game, finishing last (or tied at 1-3) regularly. The bright spots early on were Censits, Penn's first three-time All-Big 5 choice (1956-58); Bob Mlkvy, a two-time All-Big 5 performer (1960-61); the 1962-63 season; and the exciting play of Pawlak and Neuman in the mid-60s.

"It was like the Big 4 and then, 'Oh yeah, Penn too,'" recalled coach Dick Harter, who served as an assistant for seven seasons under Jack McCloskey before succeeding him in 1966. "As hard as Penn's

players and coaches tried, it was just so tough to break through with the talent at every school in Philadelphia."

That all began to change with one shot on Jan. 15, 1969, with 4,445 looking on in anticipation at a Palestra that has been the home of Penn's rich basketball history since 1927.

With 20 seconds left and the score frozen in a tie for approximately the final 7 minutes (without a shot), the inbound play was a handoff-high screen for guard Steve Bilsky. Villanova stayed in the zone it had played throughout the second half, content to let Penn hold the ball.

"We were ready, whether they stayed zone or came out and guarded us," Bilsky said. "What I didn't count on was Howard Porter, all 6-8, 6-9 of

Keven McDonald was a three-time All-Big 5 choice.

Jerome Allen (53) helped lead the Quakers to three consecutive unbeaten Ivy League seasons. Coach Dick Harter compiled an 88-44 record in five seasons.

him, popping out on me. I was supposed to roll off the pick and look to shoot, and suddenly I'm, like, 'Whoa, what are you doing out here?'"

Seven…six…five…Bilsky reverse-dribbled away from Porter and trouble…four…three . . .

"I knew I was down to seconds, and I'd moved far enough out that Porter no longer was in my face," Bilsky said. "I was able to square up and launched it, and I knew it was going in as soon as I shot it. I looked up at the clock, saw the last 2 seconds tick off and I knew we had done it."

Penn 32, Villanova 30. One of the monumental upsets in Big 5 history. No. 8 Villanova would finish 21-5. It was Penn's only Big 5 victory of a 15-10 season, but it was much more. It turned a program around.

"We were not at all established," Harter said. "That started us over the hump."

John Engles … Ron Haigler … Phil Hankinson … Michael Jordan … Matt Langel … Bruce Lefkowitz … Matt Maloney … Jack McCloskey … Keven

McDonald…

During a 25-2 season in 1969-70, the Quakers started a record 48-game, regular-season unbeaten streak that lasted until December 1971. Successive unbeaten Big 5 seasons spawned the greatest decade of dominance in Big 5 history. Seven outright or shared Big 5 titles were capped by 1978-79's storybook run to the Final Four in Bob Weinhauer's second season as head coach.

Bilsky's 25-footer had put Penn, the program without athletic scholarships, on the map in the Big 5. To stay. The Quakers went 32-8 in the Big 5 in the '70s, 223-56 overall, while also winning eight Ivy League titles.

Hardly forgotten in the midst of its run to glory was Villanova 90, Penn 47, in the NCAA East Regional final in the 1970-71 season.

It was Penn's only loss in a 28-1 season, made more difficult to swallow coming at the hands of bitter rival Villanova.

"I think of it every day," said Harter, who was so

Coach Dick Harter and his starters during the 28-1 season in 1970-71: (Bottom, from left) Corky Calhoun, Bob Morse and Jim Wolf. (Back row) Harter, Dave Wohl and Steve Bilsky.

devastated by the loss that he resigned and became head coach at Oregon. "I still can't explain it. No one can. That's your dream. You build a team and see it coming on and the quality guys you have, and then to have it come down on you like that...You should be able to handle it. I wasn't able to."

Bob Mlkvy ... Bob Morse ... Jim Murphy ... Jeff Neuman ... Ugonna Onyekwe ... Stan Pawlak ... Tony Price ... James "Booney" Salters ... George Schmidt...

Keven McDonald, a powerful, athletic, 6-8 forward who was a three-time All-Big 5 choice, had graduated and some wondered how good Penn could be without his 22.3 points per game and presence in 1978-79. Weinhauer was not one of them. Not with Tony Price, Bobby Willis, James Salters,

Matt White and Tim Smith back from a 20-8, Ivy-title winning season that ended in Providence with an 84-80 NCAA Tournament loss to Duke.

"I thought we could be something special," Weinhauer said, from his Savannah, Ga., home. "In my letter to my players that summer, I spelled it out. I wrote, 'Goals: Win the Big 5. Win the Ivy. And go to the Final Four.'"

Led by Price, who averaged 19.8 points and 8.7 rebounds, the Quakers went 25-7, 3-1 in the Big 5, and answered every challenge in advancing past Iona (73-69), North Carolina (72-71), Syracuse (84-76) and St. John's (64-62) to capture the East Regional and reach the Final Four before losing to Magic Johnson's Michigan State team, 101-67, in Salt Lake City. No Ivy League team has come close to getting back to the Final Four. It might never happen again.

Tim Smith ... Joe Sturgis ... Bob Weinhauer ... Matt White ... Bobby Willis ... Jim Wolf ... John Wideman ... Dave Wohl...

Penn basketball in the Big 5: Where to begin?

The historic Palestra, for starters.

A coaching tree (McCloskey, Harter, Daly, Weinhauer, Dunphy) comparable to any.

The players and the eras: Sturgis-Censits (late 1950s); Neuman-Pawlak (mid-1960s); Bilsky-Wohl-Calhoun-Morse (late 1960s, early '70s); McDonald-Price-White-Salters (late 1970s); Maloney-Allen (mid-1990s); Jordan-Langel (late 1990s); Koko Archibong-Onyekwe (early 2000s).

Dunphy, Penn's winningest coach with 290 victories entering his 17th season, has taken the Quakers to the NCAA Tournament eight times.

The signature years of the Dunphy era were 1992-95, when the Allen-Maloney backcourt led the Quakers to three consecutive unbeaten (42-0) Ivy League seasons and a 69-14 overall record. Those memorable years were surpassed in Penn history only by the 1969-72 seasons, when the Quakers compiled a 78-6 record with just one loss in 42 Ivy League games.

Dunphy grew up watching doubleheaders in the Palestra and played for perhaps the best team in Big 5 history, the 1968-69 La Salle powerhouse featuring Ken Durrett and Larry Cannon. When Dunphy was a senior, during the 1969-70 season, he faced a 25-2 Penn team that included Bilsky, Wohl, Calhoun and Morse. Now, as coach, the history surrounds him daily as he develops new success stories.

"I feel very, very fortunate to come full circle here," he said, "and I think there is nothing quite like the Palestra for college basketball in Philadelphia. And to be able to walk the halls and see the history every day is something special."

Bob Weinhauer was 99-45 in five seasons and led Penn to the Final Four in 1979.

Living large

SAINT JOSEPH'S HAS OVERCOME
ANY SIZE LIMITATIONS TO
ASSEMBLE A BIG-TIME PORTFOLIO

By
Dick Jerardi

The Saint Joseph's Hawk is on an endowed scholarship. Each year, there are tryouts for a position that requires a student to wear an outsized Hawk costume and flap his wings from the start of every game until its conclusion. The school's mascot is a metaphor for the passion of its fans. And passion is the best word that describes everything about St. Joe's basketball.

Since 1909 and for all 50 years of the Big 5, basketball has mattered at St. Joe's. It will matter into infinity.

They have played their on-campus home games at 3,200-seat Alumni Memorial Fieldhouse since 1949. It is a walk-in closet masquerading as a basketball court. It can be deafening, intimidating and glorious, often at the same time. It has none of the modern amenities and all of the old values. It is a gym in an era of arenas. Even though it certainly will get replaced or at least remodeled and expanded some time in the not-too-distant future, it somehow fits St. Joe's just right.

From the mid-1950s until the mid-1970s, St. Joe's played almost all its home games at the Palestra, a building that seems to make the school's defiant chant, "The Hawk Will Never Die," reverberate off the walls and ceiling. When the building is full and the Hawks are making a run at the Palestra, there really is no sound quite like it in sports. It is standing on a runway, as a jet is starting to gather speed. Only the plane never leaves.

Alumni Memorial
Fieldhouse has housed on-
campus games since 1949
and gives the Hawks a
distinct advantage.

St. Joe's still takes several of its home games to the Palestra each season and plays all its Big 5 home games there. The Hawks even play Penn on its homecourt every season, just to play another game at the Palestra. Other than Penn, no school is associated with the Palestra like St. Joe's.

If St. Joe's is a feeling, it is also a place that has produced coaches that made players, players that became coaches and one player who became bigger than life.

The "Mighty Mites" were small even for their era (1934-38). They were 54-15 under coach Bill Ferguson, the man who, in 25 seasons, won 309 games, more than any coach in St. Joe's history. Nobody knew it then, but it was the "Mighty Mites" — Matt Guokas Sr., Dan Kenney, John McMenamin, Joe Oakes and Jim Smale — who set the stage and became a metaphor for a school and a

The Hawk must be in shape, having to flap its wings throughout each game.

team that has few of the advantages but most of the will.

The Senesky brothers (George and Paul) bridged the gap to the modern era through the 1940s. George Senesky was named the Helms Foundation Player of the Year in 1942-43.

Jack Ramsay came back to his alma mater to coach in 1955 just in time for the start of the Big 5. Dr. Jack oversaw the greatest sustained period of basketball in school history and started a coaching tree that seems to have no end. Jim Lynam, Paul Westhead and Matt Guokas Jr. played for Ramsay and all went on to become NBA coaches. Jim O'Brien, Ramsay's son-in-law, played at St. Joe's after Ramsay left, but also became an NBA coach. Jack McKinney, Ramsay's assistant at St. Joe's and later the head coach there, was also an NBA coach.

Ramsay's 11 St. Joe's teams went 234-72, and 34-10 in the Big 5, including five unbeaten seasons in the City Series. In 1960-61, it was Ramsay who took St. Joe's to its only Final Four. His last two teams (1964-66) went 50-8 and set scoring records (91.1

Billy Mitchell jumped for joy at the end of stunning upset of De Paul in 1981 NCAA Tournament. Coach Jim Lynam is at left.

Cliff Anderson's No. 30 was retired on Hawk Hill.

points per game in '65-66) that will stand the test of time.

Still, it was Ramsay's innovative zone press that set him and his teams apart. It was the defense that led to him writing "Pressure Basketball," a book that is still relevant 40 years later.

Ramsay coached some of the best players in school history, including Bob McNeil, Jack Egan, Tom Wynne and Cliff Anderson, one of seven players in school history to have his jersey retired.

Just weeks after that 1961 Final Four in Kansas City, however, Ramsay had to deal with the worst moment in the school's basketball history. Three of his players — Egan, Vince Kempton and Frank Majewski — had taken money to shave points that season. When that became public, it left the school shaken to its core. Ramsay went on to greater glory, winning an NBA title with Portland in 1977, but he was haunted by the aftermath of what should have been his crowning moment at St. Joe's.

In the 29 seasons after Ramsay left, St. Joe's was sometimes good, occasionally very good, rarely bad, always competitive, but never great. Mike Bantom became the school's only Olympic basketball player in 1972. Lynam, Ramsay's point guard in 1961, orchestrated the legendary "four-to-score" upset of No. 1 De Paul in the 1981 NCAA Tournament. Norman Black, Bryan Warrick, Tony Costner, Bob Lojewski, Maurice Martin, Rodney Blake, Bernard Blunt, Rap Curry and Marvin O'Connor made certain nobody ever took St. Joe's for granted.

Five coaches followed Ramsay and his almost-impossible-to-duplicate standards. When Phil Martelli was named head coach on July 20, 1995, St. Joe's had long since faded from the national consciousness. It was a nice, regional program that could spring an upset every now and then. But that really was it.

The following March, St. Joe's was in the NIT championship game. The season after that, the Hawks won their second Atlantic 10 championship and played defending national champion Kentucky in the Sweet 16. Just like that, St. Joe's was back. And then, just as quickly, it was gone. Martelli's next three teams went 36-51. The coach was questioning everything, including himself.

Then, in 2000, a point guard from Chester High said he wanted to play for St. Joe's. In Jameer Nelson's four seasons, the Hawks went 98-28. By

Phil Martelli brought St. Joe's back to national prominence.

Jack Ramsay returned to his alma mater to coach in 1955, the first Big 5 season.

the time he left in 2004, everything about the program had changed. St. Joe's went national.

Nelson holds the school records for points, assists and steals. His No. 14 has been retired. If they ever put a statue in front of the Fieldhouse, it will be Nelson's. More than anything, he was about winning the game.

In Nelson's senior year, St. Joe's became just the second team in 25 years to finish a regular season without a loss. He was the national player of the year. Martelli was the coach of the year. On March 8, 2004, St. Joe's ascended to the No. 1 ranking for the first time in school history. The Hawks finished the season 30-2 and just seconds from the school's second Final Four.

After St. Joe's lost to Oklahoma State in the regional finals and the team was meeting in Martelli's hotel suite, Nelson, pointing toward Chris Bertolino, "The Hawk," said, "I respect the man who never stops moving his arms to show his dedication to his school."

He also said this: "All the attention I received this year as an individual, I never saw anybody get jealous. I can't ever express in words what that meant."

Nelson and his backcourt mate, Delonte West, were both selected in the first round of the 2004 NBA draft. Against the odds of modern college sports, little St. Joe's had become a major player.

After 10 seasons, Martelli (203-111) trails just Ferguson and Ramsay in career victories at the school. The coach repeatedly has said he does not want to coach anywhere else, so somewhere down the line, he will hold the wins record himself.

More important than the victories, Martelli again gave St. Joe's a cachet it had during the Ramsay era. The coach has become a national figure in his sport and has taken his program right along with him.

Later the night of the Oklahoma State loss, Martelli, knowing he was sure to get offers from bigger schools, told the players and their families: "This is my last stop. This is the job I always wanted."

Just four seasons shy of 100, St. Joe's basketball today is still about the passion. It is also about 122 wins in the last five seasons, the most wins over a half-decade in nearly 10 decades of basketball.

Matt Guokas Sr. played for the 'Mighty Mites' in the 1930s; his son, Matt, was a star guard for Jack Ramsay's Hawks in the 1960s.

Jameer Nelson set the school record for points, assists and steals, and his No. 14 has been retired.

Bench marks

LITWACK, CHANEY HAVE SET A HIGH STANDARD FOR OWLS

By
Mike Kern

Temple has had three coaches in the last half-century. And two of them — Harry Litwack and John Chaney — are enshrined in the Naismith Memorial Basketball Hall of Fame. How many schools can say that?

Nevertheless, contrary to popular belief, hoops did indeed exist on North Broad Street before the Litwack era began. After all, Temple won the first national championship and ranks seventh in college basketball history with 1,639 wins. Of those, more than 600 were achieved under 13 coaches before Litwack took over in 1952.

In 1938, Temple won the National Invitation Tournament and the national championship that went with it, what with the first NCAA Tournament still a year away.

Before Litwack took over for Josh Cody 14 years later, Bill Mlkvy, the legendary "Owl Without a Vowel," left an indelible mark on the game. In the 1950-51 season finale, he scored a school-record 73 points against Wilkes College, including 54 in a row during a 30-point win. In addition to averaging 29.2 points, a school record that still stands, he also led the nation in rebounding and finished second in assists.

Then came Litwack, "The Chief," who would go 373-193 over the next two decades. He had already been part of Temple basketball for a quarter-century, first as a player and two-time captain in the late 1920s and later as an assistant. But his tenure as the head man truly put the program out front nationally. Known as much for his cigars as his zones, he took the Owls to the Final Four in 1956 and again 2 years later. The first time, his backcourt was senior Hal Lear and sophomore Guy Rodgers, a pair of all-time lefties. All Lear did was score 745 points that season, which remains a school record. That team started 13-0. It finished 27-4, losing in the national semifinals to Iowa. In the third-place game victory against Southern Methodist, Lear closed out his

Harry Litwack put Temple basketball on the map during his long and successful tenure.

career by dropping 48. In the first round against Connecticut, Fred Cohen set an NCAA tourney record of 34 rebounds that still stands.

By the 1957-58 season, Bill "Pickles" Kennedy had replaced Lear. After losing two of their first three, the Owls won a school-best 25 in a row. Once again, they had to settle for the consolation-game win after losing by one to Kentucky in Louisville in the semis.

Litwack would make the NCAAs four more times but never advanced past the opener. In 1969, though, his Owls produced another moment in time. And this time, they cut down the nets. An 18-8, regular-season team went to the NIT, at a time when the NCAA field was still only 25 deep, and won its four games by an average of 12.5 points. The Owls beat Bob Cousy's favored Boston College club at Madison Square Garden in the final, 89-76, by scoring 25 of the last 34 points. Most folks will tell you that current Owls radio analyst John Baum was the best player in the tournament. Litwack called it "the happiest day of my coaching life." The next year, the Owls opened McGonigle Hall, an on-campus facility that seated 4,000.

In 1982, another era began, one that would sur-pass even Litwack's.

John Chaney, the Public League Player of the Year for Ben Franklin High in 1951, came to Temple from Cheyney State, where he'd won a Division II national crown 4 years earlier. His message would define the program: "Winning is an attitude." Later, that slogan became, "Be the dream." Either way, there was no denying the impact.

He, too, relied heavily on a matchup zone. And not turning the ball over. And doing more with less. His style was unique, to say the least. On and off the court. There was an edge about him that carried over to his team. It didn't take long to realize things would never be quite the same.

"There's really been a bridge between eras," Baum said. "It's like there was never any beat missed. Harry preached solid fundamentals. Nothing fancy, just basic. Coach Chaney's like that. Keep it simple, and get better and better through repetition.

"Their hallmark was defense. That came first with each man. They got the most out of what they had. Kentucky had the best players in their state. We didn't even have the best players in this city. Yet they built winning teams with what was there.

John Chaney was 499-238 entering his 24th season at Temple.

"I hear people say Chaney's not like Litwack, because he yells and curses. But you have to look through that. The approach is almost identical. Just watch. Harry had a temper. You just didn't know it was there. But we knew. If you did something wrong, he would stand up. Then he'd cross his arms. That's like John jumping up and down."

In Chaney's second season, the Owls won 26 games, their highest total since 1958, and also won an NCAA Tournament game for the first time in 26 years. In 1986-87, they went 32-4.

The following season, when the Owls were sparked by freshman guard Mark Macon, was magical. Their lone regular-season loss was by one, at Nevada-Las Vegas in late January. Two weeks later,

the Owls rose to No. 1 in the polls for the first time ever. It was also a first for a school in the Big 5 era. They would stay there the rest of the season. Only Saint Joseph's, which made it to No. 1 for the final week of the 2003-04 season, has been there, too.

On Feb. 10, in their first game after getting to No. 1, the Owls beat 20th-ranked Villanova at packed McGonigle Hall, 98-86. Howie Evans had a school record-tying 20 assists against a single turnover. The level of play on both sides was as good as it gets. Eleven days later, the Owls went to No. 5 North Carolina and won on national TV, 83-66. But the dream ended one step short of a Final Four, against Duke in the East Regional final at the Meadowlands. Chaney was recognized as the con-

Guard Guy Rodgers was a dazzling passer who played on two Final Four teams.

John Baum hoisted the championship trophy after the Ow won the NIT in 196

Freshman guard
Mark Macon led
Temple to a No. 1
ranking in 1988.

sensus top coach in the country.

The next season was the only one between 1983-84 and 2000-01 that Temple failed to make the NCAA Tournament. Beginning in 1990, the Owls made it 12 years in a row, putting them in elite company with a handful of "big-name" schools. And they made it to four more Final Eights. In none of those years (1991, '93, '99 and 2001) were they seeded higher than sixth. Each of the losses was to a No. 1 seed. And in three of them, the Owls were very much in it into the final minute. The 1993 team was led by Aaron McKie and Eddie Jones, both first-round NBA draft choices in 1994.

Along with Chaney's milestones, there have been disappointments. None hurt any more than what occurred in 2000. That March, the Owls, who had defeated No. 1 Cincinnati on the road in mid-

February, entered the NCAAs as the No. 5 team in the polls, and the second seed in the East bracket. But somehow they lost to Seton Hall, one of the last teams to get into the field, in overtime in Buffalo. Whether that group, which finished 27-6 and was led by future Olympic gold medalist Pepe Sanchez, was better than the 1987-88 contingent forever will be debated.

On Dec. 9, 1997, the Owls moved into a new, 10,000-seat home. Known then as the Apollo, it now is the Liacouras Center. The arena, located on Broad Street, wouldn't have happened without Chaney. And Chaney always has maintained he's only following the legacy Litwack left behind. So it was only right that on Nov. 21, 1999, their names were linked for posterity, at center court. Perfect together.

Chaney, at 73, is 499-238 in 23 seasons at Temple,

Perhaps the high point of the 1987-88 season came when the visiting Owls walloped No. 5 North Carolina.

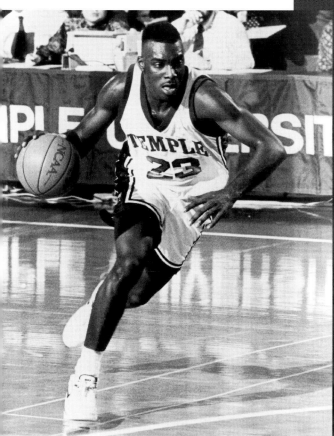

Aaron McKie played a key role in Temple's success in the 1990s.

724-297 in 33 years overall. His tenure has not been only about victories. It has been about giving an opportunity to players considered academic risks. It has been about speaking out on hot issues. And about creating controversy with his actions — like late last season, when he was suspended for five games after ordering one of his players to commit hard fouls against Saint Joseph's John Bryant.

Whatever you think of him, Chaney's place among the game's greats is secure. In 2001, he joined Litwack in the Hall of Fame. Like another

giant before him, he was humbled by the experience, a sentiment he reiterated after recording his 700th win.

"After all these years," he stressed, "I only see faces and memories of the people that gave the energy and effort responsible for bringing me here."

Tough act to follow. Which is probably what people were saying when Litwack finally called it a career.

Makes you wonder what the next 50 years might have in store.

Point guard Pepe Sanchez led the Owls to a 92-37 record.

Nova riche

WILDCATS' PROUD
HISTORY INCLUDES FAR
MORE THAN '85 TITLE

By
Dana Pennett O'Neil

The city celebrated with Villanova and Ed Pinckney when the Wildcats won the national championship in 1985.

To the collective conscious, Villanova's basketball history is easily summed up in a 2-hour window, a little game against Georgetown played on April 1, 1985.

It is the game still referred to as one of the greatest upsets in college basketball history, the one shown in celebratory film clips every March when the NCAA Tournament takes center stage, with Villanova starring as the ultimate Cinderella.

For sure, the Wildcats' improbable upset of powerful Georgetown to win the 1985 NCAA championship is the signature moment of Villanova basketball.

It is, however, the middle of Villanova's basketball story.

Not the beginning. Not the end.

"I think if you're ranking teams, you have to put Villanova in the top 15 in terms of history," said Rollie Massimino, whose coaching tenure at the school ran from the 1973-1974 season through '91-92. "The '85 team was the highlight, of course, but we had a lot of success before that and a lot after it."

Like all of Philadelphia's college basketball history books, Villanova's is thick with tradition. This is not a nouveau program, a newfangled winner that came to life 20 years ago.

Villanova has two other Final Four appearances to its credit and 1,405 wins. Those victories rank the program among the top 30 of all time, an elite list that includes the likes of Kentucky and North Carolina. Villanova's all-time roster is dotted with past greats such as Paul Arizin and Hubie White,

Three of Villanova's all-time greats: Paul Arizin (below), Bill Melchionni (right) and Howard Porter (bottom right).

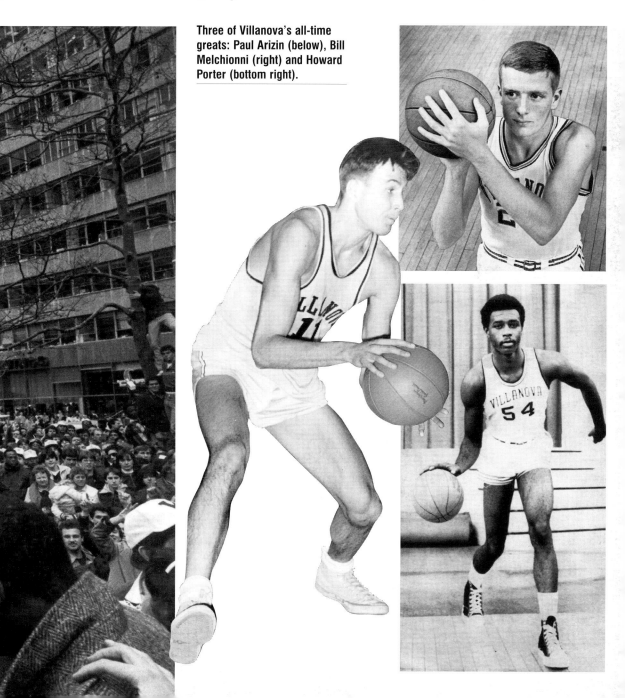

In 1973, Rollie Massimino (left) took over after the successful 12-year run of Jack Kraft (right, above).

Wali Jones and Howard Porter, alongside the more recognizable recent stars, Ed Pinckney and Kerry Kittles.

In the Big 5 annals, Villanova is everywhere. Twenty-five Wildcats are members of the Big 5 Hall of Fame, reaching as far back as Al Severance, who played at the school and later coached there from 1936 to 1961, and into the most recent history with 1997 graduate Jason Lawson.

"I think Villanova always has had a strong tradition, but when the Big 5 was formed, that really gave us a forum," said Bill Melchionni, who played from 1963 to 1966, and is one of those Big 5 Hall of Famers.

Technically, it all began in 1920, in a game against Catholic University that Villanova won, 43-40. The real beginnings of Villanova basketball, though, came in 1936 when the university hired Severance to coach.

Since then, only four other men have prowled the Villanova sideline — Jack Kraft, Massimino, Steve Lappas and Jay Wright. Each has kept the tradition

alive, winning more games than they lost.

Severance spent 25 seasons on the Main Line. Incredibly, he suffered just five losing records in that quarter of a century. In 1939 he took Villanova to its first Final Four, a smaller version of today's cash cow in which Villanova lost to Ohio State in the national semifinal.

Severance's greatest accomplishment, though, was a chance encounter in his own gym, spying a La Salle High School product who hadn't made his high school team.

His name was Paul Arizin.

Arizin would go on to score 85 points in a single game, 1,648 points in a 3-year career, earn national player of the year honors, make the All-Star team 10 times in his 12-year career with the Philadelphia Warriors, and in 1978 be inducted into the Naismith Basketball Hall of Fame.

In 1961, Severance gave way to Kraft, a man who would leave his own indelible mark on the university in his 12 seasons.

"Jack was a great guy, very fair," said Melchionni,

Curtis Sumpter (left) and Jason Fraser led Villanova deep into the 2005 NCAA Tournament.

Ed Pinckney, the center on the 1985 title team, played 14 NCAA Tournament games during his career.

Coach Al Severance was 413-201 in 25 seasons, from 1936 until 1961.

who earned All-America honors and averaged 27.6 points per game in 1965-66 under Kraft's watch. "He had a great defensive mind. I loved the way his teams played, which is what swayed me to go to Villanova."

One of the most memorable games for folks from Kraft's era was actually a Villanova loss. Fittingly it was a Big 5 game, another in the legend that has become the Holy War with Saint Joseph's. The fifth-ranked Hawks should have rolled over a 5-7 Villanova team in January 1966, the Wildcats led the entire game and seemed destined for the upset when the Hawks' sharpshooter, Billy Oakes, fouled out.

St. Joe's coach Jack Ramsay inserted seldom-used Steve Donches. As the buzzer was about to sound, Donches lofted a desperation 29-footer from the right corner.

It swished, and the Hawks prevailed, 71-69.

"I don't even like to think about that," said Melchionni, who was a senior on that team. "I can still see everybody's faces in the newspaper. It's in my brain."

Like Severance before him and Massimino after him, Kraft went to the Final Four. In 1971, Villanova met mighty UCLA in the national championship game. The Bruins were 28-1, had won 27 straight NCAA Tournament games and boasted a lineup that included Henry Bibby, Curtis Rowe and Steve Patterson.

UCLA would win its seventh national championship that year, but not before Howard Porter and the 'Cats clawed and fought before surrendering, 68-62. Later, when it was revealed that Porter had hired an agent during the season, 'Nova was stripped of its runner-up status.

Two years later, Kraft would call it quits, opening the door for a guy who had been working as an assistant at the University of Pennsylvania for 2 years, a former high school coach who loved sending his players to Villanova.

"It was my dream job," Massimino said.

Massimino struggled in his early years, so much so that he half-kiddingly told the Villanova administration that he would understand if it let him go instead of offering him a contract extension.

Everyone loves to talk about the Wildcats as the ultimate Cinderella team in 1985, implying that they were a sort of one-hit wonder. Nothing could be further from the truth. The senior class that took home the trophy had a fountain of NCAA experience to call upon. In the three previous years, they had played in eight NCAA Tournament games, including two regional finals.

Nevertheless, with its cast of role players and no real superstar against Patrick Ewing's Hoyas, it seemed like a David vs. Goliath game, which might explain why it still resonates today.

"I didn't really think it would be that big, that it would last so long," Massimino said of his team's enduring appeal.

That, despite the revelations of Gary McLain 2 years later. McLain, the point guard on the '85 team, sold the shocking story of his cocaine use that season to *Sports Illustrated*.

Since 1985, Villanova has enjoyed more successes. In 1994, the Wildcats became one of just 15 major programs to win both the NCAA and NIT championships when they defeated Vanderbilt, 80-73, for the NIT crown. A year later, Lappas' squad won the school's first Big East Conference title, defeating Connecticut, 94-78.

Last season, Villanova celebrated its 20th anniversary of the 1985 championship. The players were feted on campus, introduced to a raucous ovation during a game and then embraced at a gala in their honor that evening.

Meanwhile, the current crop of Wildcats rolled to the Sweet 16, nearly knocking out eventual national champion North Carolina.

During that game at Syracuse, the Carrier Dome stands were filled with Villanova fans. A number of them once wore Villanova basketball jerseys as well.

Wright calls his program the Villanova Family, reminding his players time and again that they are the current keepers of a great tradition, introducing them to players like Arizin and Melchionni, forging bonds steeped in basketball that can transcend generations.

"I just took out a letter Mr. and Mrs. Pinckney wrote me in 1985 about Eddie," Massimino said of his Final Four Most Outstanding Player. "It's about the kids you get. Sometimes you're lucky and sometimes you're not. But I think at Villanova we've been more lucky than not. It's about the people you get involved with; they're what make a place great."

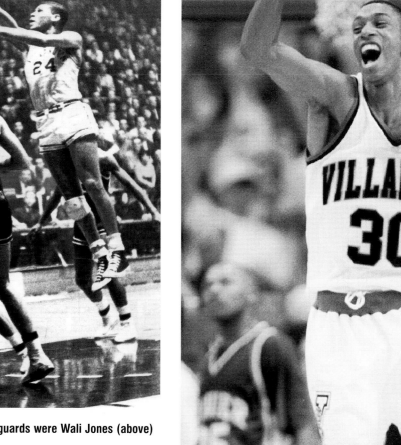

Two of Villanova's all-time guards were Wali Jones (above) and Kerry Kittles.

PHILADELPHIA BIG 5

House of hollers

THE PALESTRA HAS SEEN IT ALL: GREAT PLAYERS, MEMORABLE GAMES AND ONE BOMB SCARE

By
Robert S. Lyons

Whatever you call it — college basketball's field of dreams; the best place anywhere to watch a game; a traditional All-America shrine — there's just no facility in the world like the home of the Big 5.

"I've broadcast games in just about every arena in America, and there's nothing louder than the Palestra when it's full," said Al Meltzer, a Philadelphia sportscaster for more than 35 years who broadcast Big 5 games during the 1960s and '70s. "I can still feel the [Saint Joseph's] drum, which was always underneath the broadcasting booth. I can feel it from my toes right through the top of my head. Every time [the drummer] hit that drum, you could almost see your brain explode. You had earphones on, but it was impossible to shut the noise out. You thought that you lost your mind or something. The intensity was beyond description. You got to such a boiling point, you thought the building couldn't take it anymore. I'm surprised it's still standing."

The name Palestra was suggested by Dr. William N. Bates, a Greek professor at the University of Pennsylvania who explained that young men in ancient Greece displayed their skills in a rectangular enclosure attached to the gymnasium called a palestra.

The Palestra, located on 33rd Street on Penn's campus, opened in 1927. Since then it has held more fans at more basketball games than any other arena in the United States. In 1987, the building received a $2 million facelift that reduced its capacity from 9,240 to 8,700.

"I always tell people, whoever designed the

The Palestra, on 33rd Street on Penn's campus, was opened in 1927 for a game between the Quakers and Yale.

Palestra was a genius," said former La Salle coach Speedy Morris, who started taking his players to games there when he was coaching CYO teams in the 1960s. "I'd take a couple of kids at a time — guys who are surgeons and lawyers today — and I knew it was something they'd look forward to."

Recalled Jim Boyle, who later would play and coach at Saint Joseph's: "We had a fascination with the Palestra from the time we were kids in Southwest Philly, but we didn't have any money".

Boyle and a bunch of West Catholic High buddies like Jim Lynam and Herb Magee, who had a "burning desire" to play there, quickly discovered two ways to sneak into the building. They would scale an outside wall and climb through a window that opened underneath the scoreboard, or arrive at adjacent Hutchinson Gym well before game time and sneak through a door that opened into the Palestra.

Pat Williams, the former general manager of the 76ers and now the senior vice president of the Orlando Magic, never missed a weekend double-header at the Palestra from the beginning of the Big 5 in 1955 until he graduated from high school in Delaware in 1958.

"I had an intense love affair with the Big 5," said Williams, who still has a copy of Palestra Illustrated from every game with his ticket stub neatly stapled to the program. "To this day there is no taste or smell in the world like a boiled Palestra hot dog slathered with yellow mustard."

Just the sight of the Palestra changed the lives of some players. Dave Wohl, for example, was recruited by Penn's football program to play quarterback. One day, shortly after arriving on campus, he took a walk down 33rd Street.

"I was just looking for a place to play and walked into the Palestra," the Big 5 Hall of Fame guard

The Palestra has been home to hundreds of Big 5 games, including La Salle vs. St. Joe's in 1970.

recalled. "There was nobody in there, but to me it was just magnificent. It was the biggest thing I had ever seen at that point as a player. I just took one look at it and I was sold."

Wohl soon started making daily trips to the Palestra.

"I started playing pickup games with all the guys who had been recruited for basketball — guys like Steve Bilsky [who is Penn's athletic director] and all the seniors that I would eventually graduate with. I really liked them and started to feel, 'Hey, these are the guys I want to hang around with.' "

When Wohl informed the football coaches he had decided to concentrate on basketball, "They told me I'm probably making the biggest mistake of my life." Wohl, who played on the great Penn teams of the late 1960s and early '70s, went on to a successful NBA career spanning more than three decades as a player, coach and general manager.

Some of the world's greatest players have appeared at the Palestra against the Big 5: Oscar Robertson, of Cincinnati; Wilt Chamberlain, of Kansas; Jerry West and Rod Thorn, of West Virginia; Bill Bradley and Geoff Petrie, of Princeton; Rick Barry, of Miami; Dan Issel, of Kentucky; Julius Erving, of Massachusetts; and Calvin Murphy, of Niagara, among others.

Pete Gent, the author of "North Dallas Forty," made the Palestra all-opponent team in 1964 when he starred for Michigan State. Former Boston mayor Ray Flynn (Boston College) and NFL commissioner Paul Tagliabue (Georgetown) also played at the Palestra, as did Syracuse's Jim Brown, the great Cleveland Browns running back.

But the best of all was Bradley, the only Palestra opponent ever to be voted the Outstanding Visiting Player for three consecutive years (1963-65).

"I don't think there's a place on earth that is comparable to the Palestra," said Les Keiter, the voice of the Big 5 during the glory days of the 1960s. "I've broadcast games all over the world and no matter where I was, I would always say, 'You don't know what it's like until you walk into the Palestra.' You talk about the 'Field of Dreams' in baseball, this was my field of dreams. The mystique and the history of the place are unparalleled. When you first come through the doors there's a certain feeling that you get that just transcends the moment. Then you walk out on the floor and look up at 9,000 people, the scoreboard, the streamers, the fervor and fever in

On Dec. 6, 1930, the Palestra played host to Penn's 45-16 victory over Franklin & Marshall.

Dave Wohl was recruited by Penn to play football, but opted for basketball because of his fascination with the Palestra.

Among the collegiate greats who played at the Palestra were (from left) Jerry West, Oscar Robertson and Wilt Chamberlain.

Bill Bradley made annual visits to the Palestra for Princeton's Ivy League games against Penn.

the stands, the intensity of the players and the coaches. There's nothing like it in the world in sports. It almost defies description."

Although Keiter stayed in Philadelphia for only 6 years — he moved to Honolulu in 1970 — his name became synonymous with the Big 5. Most fans remember him for one thing.

"The first thing they say is, 'Remember the bomb scare?' I've heard that hundreds of times," Keiter said.

It only caused a 40-minute delay, but if there is a singular moment that always will live in the minds of the Big 5 fans, it's the bomb scare — Feb. 20, 1965, during halftime of the nightcap of a doubleheader featuring St. Joe's and Villanova.

The startling announcement was made over the public address system. Immediately, 9,238 fans started filing out of the building.

"I'm up in the booth high up in the rafters looking down and trying to figure out where everybody was going," Keiter recalled. "And they were all leaving their coats and their pocketbooks and their briefcases at their seats. Everyone went up the steps and filed out of the building.

"Can you imagine that? People leaving their belongings on their seats and calmly filing out? And then I suddenly saw the police and bomb squad come pouring in from all the exits. They started to search all the coats and the briefcases and pocketbooks, looking under them very gingerly. All of a sudden the police left and the people came filing back in and the game resumed."

By the way, the Hawks won, 69-61.

One of the most colorful traditions that set the Palestra apart from other college basketball arenas was the ritual enjoyed at the beginning of every game by each Big 5 school. After their team scored their first field goal, students would throw hundreds of colorful crepe paper streamers onto the floor, often completely covering the court in a sea of crimson and gray or cherry and white. Play would stop for a minute or so while the floor was cleared. For the most part, opposing coaches accepted the delay in good spirits. Then, around 1985, Princeton fans started to throw out orange and black marshmallows. Soon students in other areas of the country began abusing the privilege by tossing pieces of fruit or heavier items. Predictably, the NCAA stepped in and banned the tradition.

"I called the NCAA and requested a waiver," said Dan Baker, the former Big 5 executive director. "But they said that if they granted an exception for one school they would have to do it for others. They were afraid of injury and ruled that a technical foul should be assessed against any team whose fans throw streamers on the court."

When the NCAA ruling came down, Baker had to inform the referees working the Big 5 doubleheader that night that they would have to enforce the ban on streamers.

Penn coach Fran Dunphy and Saint Joseph's counterpart John Griffin wouldn't take no for an answer, however. After making a personal plea to the NCAA to reconsider, and being rejected, they took matters — and the Big 5 tradition — into their own hands when they matched wits in a Big 5 game on Jan. 25, 1993.

When the streamers came flying out of the stands after the Quakers scored the first basket, the officials promptly called a technical foul. But Dunphy told Andy Baratta to deliberately step over the free-throw line when he shot his foul. Rap Curry, of Saint Joseph's, was told by Griffin to do the same after Hawk fans let loose with their streamers.

A Palestra tradition lived for another day.

As the late sports writer/broadcaster Bob Vetrone once said wistfully: "If they hadn't built the Palestra, maybe there never would have been the Big 5."

Robert S. Lyons is the author of "Palestra Pandemonium: A History of the Big 5."

Les Keiter (left) broadcast the famous bomb-scare game between St. Joe's and Villanova in 1965. Al Meltzer was behind the microphone for Big 5 classics in the 1960s and 1970s.

Until the NCAA outlawed it, students would throw streamers onto the floor when their team scored its first field goal.

Behind the scenes

TWO PALESTRA CUSTODIANS MAINTAIN LIVING MUSEUM

By
Dick Jerardi

Editor's note: The following story is reprinted from "Hoops Heaven," a *Daily News* special section published on Feb. 5, 2002

Dan Harrell understands the Palestra, now in its 75th year. "It's like knowing somebody," he says. "It is like a person."

To understand a person, you need to know what's inside. Harrell, the Palestra's custodian for the last decade, knows. So does Tony Crosson, who describes himself as the Palestra's "conductor of electricity." He's been in the place for 41 years.

"And I was sneaking into games for 15 years before that."

Harrell and Crosson know every inch of the Palestra's catacombs. They walk easily through the two sets of tunnels just beyond the court. They know when walls went up and when they came down. And, yes, the building does have ghosts.

"Believe me when I tell you that there are spirits,"

Tony Crosson (left) and Dan Harrell know all the inside information on the Palestra.

Harrell says. "You can call me crazy, but I know they are here. If there are ghosts, they are pretty good guys. You see them and then they're gone. Come in by yourself and you'll see."

There is nothing, Harrell says, like being in the Palestra on a summer day at 5 a.m.

"The building," he says, "is happy with itself then."

He likes to sit in his office with his Wawa coffee and the morning paper. Then, he does the cryptogram and "listens to the ghosts play basketball."

Tour the inner sanctum of the Palestra with Tony and Dan, you get history and comedy. You find out that the old floor was laid horizontally, prompting visitors to become disoriented. Some of the old floor remains under the stands and beyond the walls. The newer, vertical floor is around 25 years old. An old picture beyond the walls reveals that there were once rowhouses where the tennis courts in front of the building are now.

Every nook and every cranny has a story. Dan tells the one about the street person he discovered inside a very tiny locker one day before a game. Dan heard something and thought it was Tony playing a joke on him. Then, he opened the locker and the man bolted out of the locker, ran through one of the tunnels and under the east stands right toward Tony.

"Tony wasn't fast enough to catch him," Dan says.

Tony did not want to catch him, Tony says.

Probably came in through "Hutch," otherwise known as Hutchinson Gym, the annex to the Palestra. Tony and Dan open a few doors, walk through some tunnels and down a very old set of wooden steps ("I know they were here 60 years ago and looking just like this," Tony says) into a vast room that they say is under Hutch.

Wilt Chamberlain fittingly was made the focal point of a section on a corridor wall devoted to Philly prep stars.

"If you got into Hutchinson Gym, you got into the Palestra," Tony says.

They show how. Back up the old stairs, down a few tunnels and through a door that now leads to the women's basketball locker room under the west stands. In those days, the door led right under the stands. There was a guard who understood what was up with all the people coming through that door. He wasn't too concerned about it.

"I don't know what you're doing here, but I think there's a seat over there," Dan quotes the guard as saying.

"[Fran] Dunphy used to sneak in through the windows," Tony says of Penn's basketball coach. "Dunphy never bought a ticket."

Now, he doesn't have to.

"I grew up in Southwest Philly, same neighborhood as Dunphy," Harrell says. "He just doesn't admit it."

Wind blows through the tunnels. Because of changes in the building through the years, air is often looking for a place to go, causing doors to slam without apparent provocation. It could be the ghosts.

Those old pictures that used to hang in the Palestra displays before the makeover in 2000? Many are now in the catacombs gathering dust, along with what has to be the original backboards,

the ones that hung from cables. Remember?

Old trophy cases and the original turnstiles are still around while somebody figures out what to do with them.

"We've got a lot of old stuff," Tony says. "We don't even know what some of it is."

Somebody did not like former President Richard Nixon. His name is all over the inside walls. He was not praised.

The wiring does not appear to be state of the art.

"It's probably illegal," Tony says. "Doesn't matter here."

There's a giant, old safe that belonged to Ogden, the concessionaires. The owner died and, according to Tony, "they never found the combination."

"Could be a lot of money in it," Tony says.

Each locker room has its own story. When Lower Merion and Kobe Bryant won the District 1 championship and earned a trip to Hershey in 1996, the team celebrated by tossing Hershey's Kisses around the locker room. They were crushed into the red carpet.

"I should get that bill and send it to Kobe," Harrell says. "He can afford it."

Harrell never liked that red carpet anyway.

"It looks like a South Philly go-go joint," he says.

Wrestlers, Dan says, are the worst.

"They like to throw things when they lose," he

The early history of Penn basketball was captured in a photo display on a corridor wall.

"...were always appreciated by well-informed fans and media."
— Dave Gavitt, Commissioner, Big East Conference

says. "It takes an extra 2 days to clean up after wrestling."

Dan points out the Palestra must have the last scoreboard where you have to go up and change the names of the teams by hand.

Just inside the women's locker room is a set of four light switches. One night not long after he started, Dan decided he should turn those lights out during a Penn-Columbia game.

"Do they look like the place where normal switches would be?" Tony asks.

No, actually, they don't. In fact, they are not normal light switches. They control the lights over the Palestra court. Dan turned them off and the building went dark while a Columbia player was attempting a jump shot.

"He walked out like he had nothing to do with it," Tony says.

"The only thing on was the scoreboard," Dan says. "It was pitch black. I snuck out and crawled under the stands."

There was the night they gave out stickers that ended up all over, sticking to everything.

"Mustard packets are the worst," Dan says. "You step on them and they squirt all over the place."

"There's millions of stories here," Tony says.

They would know. They have been there for most of them.

One of the photo displays pays tribute to the great players who have visited the Palestra.

PHILADELPHIA
BIG 5

The classics

ONE MAN'S FIVE GREATEST GAMES

By
Ed Barkowitz

The (Near) Perfect Game
April 1, 1985, at Lexington, Ky.
Villanova 66, Georgetown 64

Many people point to this as the greatest upset in an NCAA Tournament championship game. Georgetown had thrashed just about everyone during the season and looked especially dominant in drilling St. John's, 77-59, in the national semifinals.

Georgetown, which won the championship the previous season, was even stronger this year. And even though Villanova hung twice with the Hoyas during the regular season, Georgetown was peaking. Just ask the Redmen.

It would take a near-perfect game to beat Georgetown, and that's precisely what the Wildcats played.

"In the country, I don't think there were more than five people out of 250 million who would have said, 'Villanova's going to win tonight,' " said Villanova guard Harold Jensen. "I'd like to thank those people."

Trivia: Villanova hit 9 of 10 shots in the second half. Dwayne McClain was the only Wildcat to miss.

The Simmons-McCloud Game
Feb. 23, 1989, at the Palestra
La Salle 101, Florida State 100

Florida State came into the Palestra ranked 12th in the country and left with a greater appreciation of how difficult the old house could be on opponents.

The pace was frenetic from the opening tip and didn't stop until the clock read 0:00. That's no exaggeration. La Salle scored the game's first 12 points and held a 50-33 advantage at halftime.

"It was an entertaining game, great for our program," said La Salle coach Speedy Morris. "There was not a whole lot of defense played, but that's the way the fans like it."

Lionel Simmons, then a junior, had 36 points for

Harold Pressley put up a reverse layup with Georgetown's Patrick Ewing defending during Villanova's championship victory in 1985.

The celebration was just beginning as Dwayne McClain clutched the ball at the end of Villanova's victory over Georgetown in the 1985 championship game.

the Explorers. FSU bomber George McCloud matched him with 36 of his own. McCloud missed a three as time was running out that would have tied it. Teammate Tharon Mayes followed McCloud's miss with a layup that closed the scoring.

"This is the most exciting game of my career because we ran into a lot of top-ranked teams before and came up short," said La Salle's Bobby Johnson, who had 19 points. "There's no doubt about this one. It's the best one of all."

The Donches Game
Jan. 16, 1966, at the Palestra
Saint Joseph's 71, Villanova 69

The ghosts that occupy the Palestra rafters had a good time with this one.

St. Joe's entered the game 11-2 and ranked fifth in the country. Villanova was underachieving at 5-7. Naturally, they hooked up in perhaps the greatest game of the Holy War rivalry; a game that wasn't decided until an improbable player hit an improbable shot from an improbable distance.

Steve Donches, a deep reserve, was tabbed by coach Jack Ramsay to enter the game after his Hawks were riddled with foul trouble. Naturally, Donches picked up a loose ball and hit a 29-footer at the buzzer to rescue St. Joe's.

"This is only the second home game my folks have missed all year," Donches said afterward. "I didn't expect to play much, so I called them up and told them not to bother coming down. We get the Palestra games on cable TV at home. I hope they were watching."

Steve Donches (left) helped fifth-ranked St. Joe's prevail over Villanova with his buzzer-beater in 1966.

Let's Play Three
Jan. 11, 1958, at the Palestra
La Salle 111, Villanova 105

Really, does it get any better than triple overtime at the Palestra?

Villanova staged a furious rally to erase an 18-point, second-half deficit in what remains the highest-scoring Big 5 game ever.

Sophomore Bob Alden (13 points, 17 rebounds) hit a layup with 3:43 left in the third overtime that finally gave the Exlporers control of the contest. Bill Katheder's 26 points led La Salle. Tom Brennan had 29 points and 13 rebounds before fouling out for Villanova in front of a Saturday doubleheader crowd of 6,159. Saint Joseph's beat Xavier, 70-66, in an entertaining opener.

Penn Topples Goliath
March 11, 1979, at Raleigh, N.C.
Penn 72, North Carolina 71

Even though this second-round NCAA Tournament game was played at a time when Ivy League teams actually could hang with ACC teams, this victory by the Quakers was monumental. And it was a shock to everyone. Everyone, except the Quakers, that is.

"Bob Weinhauer, the Penn coach, was reasonably certain that — from a standpoint of physical talent — he had a team at least the equal of North Carolina. And one that matched up ideally," wrote *Daily News* columnist Tom Cushman. "The problem was to somehow drive this point through to the players, who have been subjected for years to the ACC's intimidating image."

The Tar Heels, who were the top seed, got 20 points from UNC legend Al Wood.

Tony Price led the ninth-seeded Quakers with 25 points, nine rebounds and six assists. A week later, the Quakers beat St. John's and advanced to the Final Four. It was the last time an Ivy League team has been to the Final Four; that's a stat that doesn't figure to change any time soon.

Five Very Honorable Mentions

March 14, 1981: Saint Joseph's knocked off No. 1 DePaul, 49-48, in an NCAA Tournament second-round game in Dayton, Ohio. Down one and with the seconds waning, Lonnie McFarlan found John Smith under the basket for the game-winning layup.

Jan. 4, 1990: Bo Kimble's 35-footer at the buzzer was the difference as Loyola Marymount sank Saint Joseph's, 99-96, in a game at Hawk Hill. Kimble finished with 54 points, a record for a Big 5 opponent.

Feb. 25, 1984: Ralph Lewis and La Salle upset

Lionel Simmons threw down 36 points when La Salle outscored Florida State, 101-100, in 1989.

St. Joe's John Smith was hugged by Jeffery Clark after his layup sank top-ranked DePaul in the 1981 NCAA Tournament.

Temple, 80-79, in double overtime. Lewis forced the first overtime when he hit a clutch shot and then blocked a Terence Stansbury jumper with 1 second remaining in regulation. Stansbury responded by hitting a 25-footer at the buzzer to force the second overtime. But Lewis had the last word with two free throws to seal it in double OT.

March 3, 2002: Lynn Greer's three-point play with 1.2 seconds left in double overtime lifted Temple over Saint Joseph's, 87-84.

"That was as good as it gets," St. Joe's coach Phil Martelli said. "Terrific teams, terrific individual performances. An exceptional game."

Remember, that was the *losing* coach.

Feb. 26, 1983: John Pinone's off-balance 18-footer at the buzzer gave Villanova a 71-70 overtime win over St. John's and a share of the Big East regular-season title.

Tony Price (left) scored 25 points when Penn stunned North Carolina in the 1979 NCAA Tournament. Lynn Greer (above) launched a shot that propelled Temple over St. Joe's in double overtime in 2002.

PHILADELPHIA
BIG 5

It's debatable

ONE MAN'S BIG 5 TOP 50

By
Kevin Mulligan

Editor's note: The following story is reprinted from the *Daily News* published on March 31, 2005

Let the arguments and debates begin as we present our 50 greatest Big 5 players in celebration of the 50th anniversary of the Big 5. May the discussion last until next winter, when the Big 5 will select an official 50 greatest players list based on nominations from the schools. Our choices took 4 weeks of teeth-grinding, hair-splitting research and the ever-difficult comparison of Big 5 eras. Legends galore didn't make it and we offer apologies in advance. This list has been pared from an original checklist of 113 we considered worthy. That's how tough it was. Rather than involve several friends I consider "authorities" in a survey that may only have made the process more grueling, I tapped into just one legend, the late Bob Vetrone, who saw all of them play from 1955-present. (I started watching Big 5 games in 1963.) He helped me with my final (and impossible) cut from 68 to 50 shortly before he left us last week. He kept his promise of keeping this a secret, and sadly, he never got around to listing his personal top 50. "After 25, it's ridiculous," he said. So true.

This was not driven exclusively by statistics or honors, and pro careers were not a factor. We rated team players well ahead of selfish gunners, few of whom made the list. In the end, preference was given to the Big 5 heyday of the 1960s and '70s, when there were arguably 15 bona fide All-Big 5-caliber stars each year in the city. Our 50 share one thing: greatness; not "very goodness." And I still can't get over the names who didn't survive the final cut, many of them three-time All-Big 5 choices, 2,000-point scorers and personal friends and favorites. Enjoy the memories.

Villanova's 1970-71 team featured the likes of (from left) Howard Porter, Hank Siemiontkowski and Chris Ford.

Two greats from the 1960s were St. Joe's Cliff Anderson (above) and Villanova's Hubie White.

1 KEN DURRETT
La Salle
Consensus All-America, 1971; best player of his era; power, athleticism, relentless scorer, rebounder; guard skills in 6-8 forward's body; three-time Big 5 MVP, 1969-71; 1,679 career points (3 seasons); 27.0 points per game, 12.0 rebounds per game in 21 games as a senior, before suffering a torn ACL.

2 HOWARD PORTER
Villanova
Three-time All-America, 1969-71; Final Four MVP, 1971; Big 5 MVP, 1969; 2,026 points tops 3-year Big 5 players (no varsity as freshman); school-record 22.8 career ppg.

3 CLIFF ANDERSON
St. Joe's
1967 All-America, three-time first-team Big 5; Big 5 MVP, '67; 1,728 points (3 years).

4 GUY RODGERS
Temple
Three-time Big 5 MVP, 1956-58; consensus All-America, '57, '58; 1,767 points; assist wizard.

5 JAMEER NELSON
St. Joe's
2004 National Player of the Year, All-America; 2,094 points, 713 assists; four-time Big 5 first-teamer.

6 LIONEL SIMMONS
La Salle
1990 National Player of Year; three-time Big 5 MVP, 1988-90); Big 5's all-time scoring leader, 3,217 points (4 years); 1,429 rebounds; career averages of 24.6 ppg, 10.6 rpg.

7 HUBIE WHITE
Villanova
1962 Look Magazine, U.S. Basketball Writers All-America, Big 5 MVP; three-time All-Big 5, 1960-62. The best of the early-era big guards who also played forward; 1,608 career points (20.6 average).

8 MICHAEL BROOKS
La Salle
1980 National Player of the Year; All-America, 1980; 4-year first-team Big 5; Big 5 MVP, 1978 and '80; 1980 Olympian (boycott); career 2,628 points (23.1), 1,372 rebounds (12.8).

9 WALI JONES
Villanova
All-America, 1964; two-time Big 5 MVP, 1963 and '64; three-time All-Big 5; 16.8 career ppg.

Corky Calhoun was a key player on Penn's powerful teams in the early 1970s.

10 LARRY CANNON
La Salle
Three-time Big 5 first-teamer, 1967-69; 1,430 points.

11 MATT GUOKAS
St. Joe's
Consensus All-America, 1966; two-time All-Big 5 after transfer from Miami.

12 BILL MELCHIONNI
Villanova
1966 All-America and Big 5 MVP; two-time All-Big 5, NIT MVP, 1966; 1,612 career points (19.2).

13 BOBBY McNEILL
St. Joe's
1960 All-America; North Catholic legend joined Guy Rodgers and Hal Lear among best guards of the 1950s; All-Big 5, 1958-60.

14 CORKY CALHOUN
Penn
Big 5 MVP, 1972, All-Big 5, 1970-72.

15 ED PINCKNEY
Villanova
Big 5 MVP and Final 4 Most Outstanding Player, 1985; three-time All-Big 5, 1983-85.

16 BILL "PICKLES" KENNEDY
Temple
Another Rodgers mate; carried Owls post-Rodgers; Big 5 MVP, 1960.

17 JOHN BAUM
Temple
First-team Big 5, 1967-69; led Temple to NIT title in '69.

18 MIKE HAUER
St. Joe's
Three-time All-Big 5 first team, 1968-70; arguably toughest 6-4 center in Big 5 history.

19 JOHNNY JONES
Villanova
Big 5 MVP in one of its greatest seasons, 1967-68; three-time All-Big 5 first team; stood 6-4, played about 6-10.

20 TOM INGELSBY
Villanova
1973 Big 5 MVP; two-time All-Big 5, one of great shooters in Big 5 history; 1,616 career points (18.6), 3 years.

Villanova's John Pinone was a Big 5 MVP three times, from 1981-83.

Bill 'Pickles' Kennedy
was the Big 5 MVP
in 1960.

21 JIM WASHINGTON
Villanova
Three-time All-Big 5 forward, 1963-65; Big 5 MVP, '65.

22 MARK MACON
Temple
Rare four-time Big 5 first-teamer; 2,609 points; 1988 All-America for No. 1-ranked, 32-2, Elite 8 Owls.

23 MIKE BANTOM
St. Joe's
1973 All-America; U.S. Olympian, 1972; two-time first-team Big 5.

24 JOHN PINONE
Villanova
Big 5 MVP, 1981-83; third-team All-America, 1983; four-time All-Big 5; 2,204 points.

25 DICK CENSITS
Penn
First three-time All-Big 5 pick, 1956-58.

26 CHRIS FORD
Villanova
Flashy leader of Final Four 'Cats in 1971; 15.7 career ppg; 500 career assists (3 years); co-MVP with Calhoun, 1972.

St. Joe's Mike Bantom was a two-time first-team Big 5 player and a member of the U.S. Olympic team in 1972.

Granger Hall provided a powerful inside presence for Temple in the 1980s.

27 PEPE SANCHEZ
Temple
Three-time Big 5 first team, 1998-2000; two-time MVP, 1999, 2000; Basketball Times first-team All-America, '00; national steals leader, 1999 and 2000.

28 RON HAIGLER
Penn
Often compared to Howard Porter; two-time Big 5 MVP, '74 and '75; Ivy player of year, '75.

29 KERRY KITTLES
Villanova
Consensus first-team All-America, 1996; Big 5 MVP, 1995 and '96; Big East player of year, '95; school's all-time scoring leader (2,243 points).

30 AARON McKIE
Temple
Big 5 MVP, 1993; three-time All-Big 5 (1992-94); Atlantic 10 player of year, '93.

31 EDDIE JONES
Temple
Big 5 MVP, Atlantic 10 player of year, 1994; two-time All-Big 5; also great defensive player.

32 BERNIE WILLIAMS
La Salle
Great shooting guard; 16.6 career average in huge shadow of Durrett-Cannon in late 1960s.

33 HAL LEAR
Temple
Played just one year in the Big 5, its first (1955-56), but no list of legends would be complete without Rodgers' prolific scoring partner (745 points in 1955-56 season).

34-35 (Entry) STEVE BILSKY, DAVE WOHL
Penn
Neither made All-Big 5 due to depth of Big 5 talent, 1968-71. They are synonymous with great Big 5 guard play and dribbling out victories for Quakers.

36 RODNEY BLAKE
St. Joe's
Big 5 first team, 1986-88; four-time All-Atlantic 10; 1,679 points; all-time blocked-shot leader (419) in Big 5.

37 FRANK CORACE
La Salle
All-Big 5, 1963 and '64; one of dominant forwards of the early '60s; 1,411 points (19.3 ppg).

38 JAY NORMAN
Temple
Mr. Inside, at just 6-3, for Temple's Final Four teams in late '50s.

39 BOBBY MORSE
Penn
All-Big 5 shooting forward, 1971 and '72; might have scored 2,000 if there was a three-point arc.

40 BRUCE DRYSDALE
Temple
Big 5 MVP, 1961, two-time All-Big 5.

41 JACK EGAN
St. Joe's
1,363 points, 871 rebounds in just 83 games, 1958-61.

42 KEITH HERRON
Villanova
Three-year All-Big 5, 1976-78; dominated big men at just 6-6.

43 KEVEN McDONALD
Penn
Big 5 MVP, 1977; unstoppable, powerfully built 6-5 scorer; three-time All-Big 5, 1976-78.

44 GRANGER HALL
Temple
All-Big 5, 1982, '84 and '85; dominant power player.

45 JIM HUGGARD
Villanova
All-Big 5 first team, 1959-61; 15.8 career ppg; amazing passer.

46 HUBIE MARSHALL
La Salle
Explosive, powerful scoring guard; All-Big 5, 1966 and '67.

47 DAN KELLY
St. Joe's
All-Big 5, 1968 and '70; 1,524 points; floor general extraordinaire.

48 HANK SIEMIONTKOWSKI
Villanova
1972 All-America; 6-6 shooter, punishing rebounder on 1971 Final Four team.

49 JIM LYNAM
St. Joe's
Big 5 co-MVP (with Wali Jones), 1963; one of the elite Big 5 lead guards of early '60s.

50 MAURICE MARTIN
St. Joe's
All-Big 5 do-everything 6-6 guard, 1984-86; A-10 player of year, 1986.

Frank Corace averaged 19.3 points for La Salle in the 1960s.

PHILADELPHIA BIG 5

Records

By
Bob Vetrone Jr.

TEAMS AT A GLANCE

LA SALLE

Best Records: 30-2 (1989-90); 23-1 (1968-69); 26-6 (1988-89).
Best pre-Big 5 Record: 25-3 (1952-53).
Worst Record: 6-24 (1995-96).
NCAA Tournament Record: 11-10 in 11 appearances.
Best NCAA Finishes: Won title (1954); Lost in final (1955).
NIT Record: 9-10 in 11 appearances.
Best NIT Finishes: Won title (1952); Lost in final (1987).

PENN

Best Records: 28-1 (1970-71); 25-2 (1969-70); 25-3 (1971-72, 1993-94).
Best pre-Big 5 Record: 22-1 (1919-20).
Worst Record: 7-19 (1956-57).
NCAA Tournament Record: 13-23 in 21 appearances.
Best NCAA Finishes: Lost in semi-final (1979); Lost in regional finals (1971, 1972).
NIT Record: 0-1 in 1 appearance.
Best NIT Finishes: Lost in first round (1981).

SAINT JOSEPH'S

Best Records: 30-2 (2003-04); 26-3 (1964-65); 25-5 (1960-61, 1981-82).
Best pre-Big 5 Record: 14-1 (1914-15).
Worst Record: 7-21 (1989-90).
NCAA Tournament Record: 18-22 in 18 appearances.
Best NCAA Finishes: Lost in semi-final (1961); Lost in regional finals (1963, 1981, 2004).
NIT Record: 15-13 in 13 appearances.
Best NIT Finishes: Lost in final (1996, 2005); Lost in semifinals (1956).

TEMPLE

Best Records: 32-2 (1987-88); 32-4 (1986-87); 27-3 (1957-58).
Best pre-Big 5 Record: 23-2 (1937-38).
Worst Record: 6-19 (1958-59).
NCAA Tournament Record: 31-25 in 25 appearances.
Best NCAA Finishes: Lost in semi-finals (1956, 1958); Lost in regional finals (1944, 1988, 1991, 1993, 1999, 2001).
NIT Record: 20-14 in 16 appearances.
Best NIT Finishes: Won titles (1938, 1969); Lost in semifinals (1957, 2002).

VILLANOVA

Best Records: 24-4 (1963-64); 23-5 (1964-65); 26-7 (1995-96).
Best pre-Big 5 Record: 19-2 (1939-40).
Worst Record: 7-19 (1973-74).
NCAA Tournament Record: 39-26 in 26 appearance.
Best NCAA Finishes: Won title (1985); Lost in final (1971); Lost in semifinal (1939).
NIT Record: 24-17 in 17 appearances.
Best NIT Finishes: Won title (1994); Lost in final (1965); Lost in semifinals (1963, 1966, 1977).

OVERALL WON-LOST RECORDS

Season	La Salle W-L	Penn W-L	SJU W-L	Temple W-L	Villanova W-L
1955-56	15-10	12-13	23-6	27-4	14-12
1956-57	17-9	7-19	17-7	20-9	10-15
1957-58	16-9	13-12	18-9	27-3	12-11
1958-59	16-7	12-14	22-5	6-19	18-7
1959-60	16-6	14-11	20-7	17-9	20-6
1960-61	15-7	16-9	25-5	20-8	11-13
1961-62	16-9	17-8	18-10	18-9	21-7
1962-63	16-8	19-6	23-5	15-7	19-10
1963-64	16-9	14-10	18-10	17-8	24-4
1964-65	15-8	15-10	26-3	14-10	23-5
1965-66	10-15	19-6	24-5	21-7	18-11
1966-67	14-12	11-14	16-10	20-8	17-9
1967-68	20-8	9-17	17-9	19-9	19-9
1968-69	23-1	15-10	17-11	22-8	21-5
1969-70	14-12	25-2	15-12	15-13	22-7
1970-71	20-7	28-1	19-9	13-12	23-6
1971-72	6-19	25-3	19-9	23-8	20-8
1972-73	15-10	21-7	22-6	17-10	11-14
1973-74	18-10	21-6	19-11	16-9	7-19
1974-75	22-7	23-5	8-17	7-19	9-18
1975-76	11-15	17-9	10-16	9-18	16-11
1976-77	17-12	18-8	13-13	17-11	23-10
1977-78	18-12	20-8	13-15	24-5	23-9
1978-79	15-13	25-7	19-11	25-4	15-13
1979-80	22-9	17-12	21-9	14-12	23-8
1980-81	14-13	20-8	25-8	20-8	20-11
1981-82	16-13	17-10	25-5	19-8	24-8
1982-83	18-14	17-9	15-13	14-15	24-8
1983-84	20-11	10-16	20-9	26-5	19-12
1984-85	15-13	13-14	19-12	25-6	25-10
1985-86	14-14	15-11	26-6	25-6	23-14
1986-87	20-13	13-14	16-13	32-4	15-16
1987-88	24-10	10-16	15-14	32-2	24-13
1988-89	26-6	13-13	8-21	18-12	18-16
1989-90	30-2	12-14	7-21	20-11	18-15
1990-91	19-10	9-17	13-17	24-10	17-15
1991-92	20-11	16-10	13-15	17-13	14-15
1992-93	14-13	22-5	18-11	20-13	8-19
1993-94	11-16	25-3	14-14	23-8	20-12
1994-95	13-14	22-6	17-12	19-11	25-8
1995-96	6-24	17-10	19-13	20-13	26-7
1996-97	10-17	12-14	26-7	20-11	24-10
1997-98	9-18	17-12	11-17	21-9	12-17
1998-99	13-15	21-6	12-18	24-11	21-11
1999-00	11-17	21-8	13-16	27-6	20-13
2000-01	12-17	12-17	26-7	24-13	18-13
2001-02	15-17	25-7	19-12	19-15	19-13
2002-03	13-16	22-6	23-7	18-16	15-16
2003-04	10-20	17-10	30-2	15-14	18-17
2004-05	10-19	20-9	24-12	16-14	24-8

CITY SERIES WON-LOST RECORDS

Season	La Salle (Pos.) W-L	Penn (Pos.) W-L	SJU (Pos.) W-L	Temple (Pos.) W-L	Villanova (Pos.) W-L
1955-56	(3) 2-2	(5) 0-4	(1) 4-0	(2) 3-1	(4) 1-3
1956-57	(t1) 3-1	(5) 0-4	(t1) 3-1	(t1) 3-1	(4) 1-3
1957-58	(3) 1-3	(3) 1-3	(2) 3-1	(1) 4-0	(3) 1-3
1958-59	(3) 1-3	(3) 1-3	(1) 4-0	(3) 1-3	(2) 3-1
1959-60	(4) 1-3	(3) 2-2	(t1) 3-1	(4) 1-3	(t1) 3-1
1960-61	(3) 2-2	(4) 1-3	(1) 4-0	(2) 3-1	(5) 0-4
1961-62	(t2) 2-2	(t4) 1-3	(t4) 1-3	(t2) 2-2	(1) 4-0
1962-63	(t4) 1-3	(t1) 3-1	(3) 2-2	(t4) 1-3	(t1) 3-1
1963-64	(1) 3-1	(5) 1-3	(t2) 2-2	(t2) 2-2	(t2) 2-2
1964-65	(t2) 2-2	(5) 0-4	(1) 4-0	(t2) 2-2	(t2) 2-2
1965-66	(4) 1-3	(3) 2-2	(1) 4-0	(2) 3-1	(5) 0-4
1966-67	(4) 1-3	(5) 0-4	(3) 2-2	(2) 3-1	(5) 4-0
1967-68	(t2) 2-2	(4) 1-3	(1) 3-1	(t2) 2-2	(t2) 2-2
1968-69	(1) 4-0	(t4) 1-3	(t4) 1-3	(t2) 2-2	(t2) 2-2
1969-70	(5) 0-4	(1) 4-0	(3) 2-2	(4) 1-3	(2) 3-1
1970-71	(t2) 2-2	(1) 4-0	(t2) 2-2	(5) 0-4	(t2) 2-2
1971-72	(5) 0-4	(t1) 3-1	(t3) 2-2	(t1) 3-1	(t3) 2-2
1972-73	(t4) 1-3	(1) 4-0	(t2) 2-2	(t2) 2-2	(t4) 1-3
1973-74	(t2) 2-2	(1) 4-0	(t2) 2-2	(t2) 2-2	(5) 0-4
1974-75	(1) 4-0	(2) 3-1	(5) 0-4	(4) 1-3	(3) 2-2
1975-76	(t4) 1-3	(3) 2-2	(t1) 3-1	(t4) 1-3	(t1) 3-1
1976-77	(t3) 2-2	(t1) 3-1	(5) 0-4	(t1) 3-1	(t3) 2-2
1977-78	(t3) 2-2	(t3) 2-2	(5) 0-4	(t1) 3-1	(t1) 3-1
1978-79	(t4) 1-3	(t1) 3-1	(3) 2-2	(t1) 3-1	(t4) 1-3
1979-80	(t3) 1-3	(t3) 1-3	(1) 4-0	(t3) 1-3	(2) 3-1
1980-81	(t1) 2-2	(t1) 2-2	(t1) 2-2	(t1) 2-2	(t1) 2-2
1981-82	(t4) 1-3	(t4) 1-3	(t1) 3-1	(t1) 3-1	(3) 2-2
1982-83	(5) 1-3	(t2) 2-2	(t2) 2-2	(t2) 2-2	(1) 3-1
1983-84	(t1) 3-1	(5) 0-4	(t3) 2-2	(t1) 3-1	(t3) 2-2
1984-85	(t2) 2-2	(5) 0-4	(t2) 2-2	(t2) 2-2	(1) 4-0
1985-86	(t4) 1-3	(t4) 1-3	(t1) 3-1	(t1) 3-1	(3) 2-2
1986-87	(t2) 2-2	(5) 0-4	(t2) 2-2	(1) 4-0	(t2) 2-2
1987-88	(5) 0-4	(4) 1-3	(2) 3-1	(1) 4-0	(3) 2-2
1988-89	(t1) 3-1	(t4) 1-3	(t4) 1-3	(t1) 3-1	(3) 2-2
1989-90	(1) 4-0	(5) 0-4	(4) 1-3	(3) 2-2	(2) 3-1
1990-91	(t3) 2-2	(5) 0-4	(t1) 3-1	(t1) 3-1	(t3) 2-2
1991-92	(t1) 1-1	(t1) 1-1	(t1) 1-3	(t1) 1-1	(t1) 1-1
1992-93	(t2) 1-1	(t2) 1-1	(t2) 1-3	(1) 2-0	(5) 0-2
1993-94	(t4) 0-2	(t1) 2-0	(t4) 0-2	(t1) 2-0	(2) 1-1
1994-95	(t4) 0-2	(t4) 0-2	(t1) 2-0	(t1) 2-0	(3) 1-1
1995-96	(5) 0-2	(t2) 1-3	(t2) 1-1	(1) 2-0	(t2) 1-1
1996-97	(t4) 0-2	(t4) 0-2	(3) 1-1	(t1) 2-0	(t1) 2-0
1997-98	(t1) 1-1	(t1) 1-1	(t1) 1-1	(t1) 1-1	(t1) 1-1
1998-99	(t2) 1-1	(t2) 1-1	(5) 0-2	(t2) 1-1	(1) 2-0
1999-00	(3) 2-2	(t4) 1-3	(t4) 1-3	(t1) 3-1	(t1) 3-1
2000-01	(t2) 2-2	(5) 0-4	(t2) 2-2	(t2) 2-2	(1) 4-0
2001-02	(t2) 2-2	(1) 4-0	(t4) 1-3	(t4) 1-3	(t2) 2-2
2002-03	(5) 0-4	(2) 3-1	(1) 4-0	(4) 1-3	(3) 2-2
2003-04	(5) 0-4	(4) 1-3	(1) 4-0	(3) 2-2	(2) 3-1
2004-05	(5) 0-4	(t3) 2-2	(t3) 2-2	(t1) 3-1	(t1) 3-1

CITY SERIES AT A GLANCE

LA SALLE

City Series Titles: 10 (4 outright)
Perfect (4-0) Seasons: 3 (last: 1989-90)
Longest Winning Streak: 6 (ended: Jan. 17, 1976)
Longest Losing Streak: 12 (current)
All-Time Record: 73-111
Most Points, Game:
40, Steve Black (Feb. 26, 1983, vs. Temple)

PENN

City Series Titles: 13 (5 outright)
Perfect (4-0) Seasons: 5 (last: 2001-02)
Longest Winning Streak: 12 (ended: Jan. 18, 1975)
Longest Losing Streak: 12 (ended: Jan. 19, 1992)
All-Time Record: 73-111
Most Points, Game:
37, Stan Pawlak (Jan. 12, 1966, vs. La Salle)

SAINT JOSEPH'S

City Series Titles: 19 (9 outright)
Perfect (4-0) Seasons: 8 (last: 2003-04)
Longest Winning Streak: 10 (ended: Jan. 28, 1967)
Longest Losing Streak: 10 (ended: Feb. 9, 1979)
All-Time Record: 104-80
Most Points, Game:
37, Marvin O'Connor (March 3, 2001, vs. La Salle)

TEMPLE

City Series Titles: 23 (5 outright)
Perfect (4-0) Seasons: 3 (last: 1987-88)
Longest Winning Streak: 10 (ended: Dec. 16, 1997)
Longest Losing Streak: 7 (ended: Dec. 18, 1971)
All-Time Record: 108-76
Most Points, Game:
37, Hal Lear (Jan. 11, 1956, vs. Villanova)

VILLANOVA

City Series Titles: 16 (6 outright)
Perfect (4-0) Seasons: 4 (last: 2000-01)
Longest Winning Streak: 7 (ended: Nov. 27, 2001)
Longest Losing Streak: 7 (ended: Jan. 25, 1975)
All-Time Record: 102-82
Most Points, Game:
39, Tom Sienkiewicz (Feb. 13, 1979, vs. Penn)

COACHES IN THE BIG 5 ERA

School	Coach	First Season	Yrs.	W- L	Pct.
Villanova	*Al Severance	1936-37	25	413-201	.673
Temple	*Harry Litwack	1952-53	21	373-193	.654
Penn	*Ray Stanley	1954-55	2	31- 19	.620
La Salle	Jim Pollard	1955-56	3	48- 28	.632
Saint Joseph's	Jack Ramsay	1955-56	11	234- 72	.765
Penn	Jack McCloskey	1956-57	10	146-105	.582
La Salle	Dudey Moore	1958-59	5	79- 37	.681
Villanova	Jack Kraft	1961-62	12	238- 95	.715
La Salle	Bob Walters	1963-64	2	31- 17	.646
La Salle	Joe Heyer	1965-66	2	24- 27	.471
Penn	Dick Harter	1966-67	5	88-44	.667
Saint Joseph's	Jack McKinney	1966-67	8	144- 77	.652
La Salle	Jim Harding	1967-68	1	20- 8	.714
La Salle	Tom Gola	1968-69	2	37- 13	.760
La Salle	Paul Westhead	1970-71	9	142-105	.575
Penn	Chuck Daly	1971-72	6	125- 38	.767
Temple	Don Casey	1973-74	9	151- 94	.616
Villanova	Rollie Massimino	1973-74	19	357-241	.597
Saint Joseph's	Harry Booth	1974-75	4	44- 61	.419
Penn	Bob Weinhauer	1977-78	5	99- 45	.688
Saint Joseph's	Jim Lynam	1978-79	3	65- 28	.699
La Salle	Lefty Ervin	1979-80	7	110- 87	.558
Saint Joseph's	Jim Boyle	1981-82	9	151-114	.570
Penn	Craig Littlepaige	1982-83	3	40- 39	.506
Temple	John Chaney	1982-83	23	499-238	.677
Penn	Tom Schneider	1985-86	4	51- 54	.486
La Salle	Speedy Morris	1986-87	15	238-203	.540
Penn	Fran Dunphy	1989-90	16	290-154	.653
Saint Joseph's	John Griffin	1990-91	5	75- 69	.521
Villanova	Steve Lappas	1992-93	9	174-110	.613
Saint Joseph's	Phil Martelli	1995-96	10	203-111	.646
La Salle	Billy Hahn	2001-02	3	37- 54	.407
Villanova	Jay Wright	2001-02	4	76- 54	.585
La Salle	John Giannini	2004-05	1	10- 19	.345

*Records from 1955-56 on: Severance 85-64, Litwack 331-161, Stanley 12-13.

Jay Wright had a record of 76-54 in his first four seasons at Villanova.

Penn's Chuck Daly (left) and Temple's Don Casey shared a laugh with former Owls coach Harry Litwack before their teams met in 1975.

BIG 5 MEN'S HALL OF FAME

PLAYERS (110)

Cliff Anderson (SJ, 1973)
Paul Arizin (V, 2000)
Mike Bantom (SJ, 1979)
John Baum (T, 1978)
Ernie Beck (P, 2000)
Bob Bigelow (P, 1989)
Steve Bilsky (P, 1988)
Norman Black (SJ, 1985)
Steve Black (LS, 1992)
Nate Blackwell (T, 1993)
Rodney Blake (SJ, 1994)
Bernard Blunt (SJ, 2001)
Jim Boyle (SJ, 1997)
Alex Bradley (V, 1987)
Clarence Brookins (T, 1984)
Michael Brooks (LS, 1986)
Joe Bryant (LS, 1981)
Corky Calhoun (P, 1976)
Larry Cannon (LS, 1973)
Dick Censits (P, 1981)
Jeffery Clark (SJ, 1996)
Tim Claxton (T, 1987)
Frank Corace (LS, 1974)
Tony Costner (SJ, 1990)
Steve Courtin (SJ, 1980)
Jim Crawford (LS, 1993)
Bruce Drysdale (T, 1977)
Ken Durrett (LS, 1975)
Kurt Engelbert (SJ, 1986)
John Engles (P, 1995)
Howard Evans (T, 1994)
Bob Fields (LS, 1984)
Chris Ford (V, 1977)
Tom Gola (LS, 2000)
Stewart Granger (V, 1990)
Chip Greenberg (LS, 2003)
Matt Guokas Jr. (SJ, 1976)
Ron Haigler (P, 1982)
Granger Hall (T, 1991)
Phil Hankinson (P, 1980)
Mike Hauer (SJ, 1977)
Keith Herron (V, 1984)
Jim Huggard (V, 1978)
Jack Hurd (LS, 1999)
Tom Ingelsby (V, 1979)
Harold Jensen (V, 1995)
Ollie Johnson (T, 1979)
Eddie Jones (T, 2002)
Johnny Jones (V, 1981)
Wali Jones (V, 1973)
Dan Kelly (SJ, 1980)
Bill Kennedy (T, 1975)
Mik Kilgore (T, 1998)
Jason Lawson (V, 2004)
Hal Lear (T, 1974)

Tim Legler (LS, 1995)
Alonzo Lewis (LS, 1980)
Ralph Lewis (LS, 1991)
Bob Lojewski (SJ, 1998)
Jim Lynam (SJ, 1975)
Mark Macon (T, 1997)
Hubie Marshall (LS, 1977)
Maurice Martin (SJ, 1992)
Bob McAteer (LS, 1976)
Dwayne McClain (V, 1993)
Keven McDonald (P, 1985)
Pat McFarland (SJ, 1984)
Aaron McKie (T, 2002)
Bob McNeill (SJ, 1974)
Bill Melchionni (V, 1974)
Bill Mlkvy (T, 2000)
Bob Mlkvy (P, 1998)
Bob Morse (P, 1977)
Jeff Neumann (P, 1984)
Jay Norman (T, 1976)
Jim O'Brien (SJ, 1989)
Doug Overton (LS, 1997)
Stan Pawlak (P, 1973)
Tim Perry (T, 1994)
Ed Pinckney (V, 1991)
John Pinone (V, 1989)
Howard Porter (V, 1981)
Harold Pressley (V, 1992)
Tony Price (P, 1985)
Guy Rodgers (T, 1973)
Joe Ryan (V, 1991)
George Senesky (SJ, 2000)

Hank Siemiontkowski (V, 1988)
Lionel Simmons (LS, 1996)
Tim Smith (P, 1999)
Rory Sparrow (V, 1986)
Joe Spratt (SJ, 1983)
Terence Stansbury (T, 1990)
Joe Sturgis (P, 1983)
Bill Taylor (LS, 1989)
Roland Taylor (LS, 2005)
Mike Vreeswyk (T, 1995)
Bryan Warrick (SJ, 1988)
Jim Washington (V, 1975)
Doug West (V, 1996)
Hubie White (V, 1976)
John Wideman (P, 1974)
Alvin Williams (V, 2003)
Bernie Williams (LS, 1982)
Boo Williams (SJ, 1987)
Jim Williams (T, 1983)
Charlie Wise (LS, 1982)
Dave Wohl (P, 1975)
Randy Woods (LS, 1998)
Tom Wynne (SJ, 1978)

COACHES (10)

Chuck Daly (P, 2001)
Tom Gola (LS, 1986)
Dick Harter (P, 1993)
Jack Kraft (V, 1987)
Harry Litwack (T, 1978)
Jack McCloskey (P, 1994)
Jack McKinney (SJ, 1992)

Jack Ramsay (SJ, 1983)
Al Severance (V, 1994)
Bob Weinhauer (P, 2002)

ADMINISTRATIVE (15)

Dan Baker (Executive secretary, 1997)
Ernie Casale (Temple athletic director, 1982)
Andy Dougherty (Saint Joseph's sports information director, 1989)
Les Keiter (Broadcaster, 2003)
Bob McKee (Official scorer, 1990)
Al Meltzer (Television, 1993)
John Nash (Executive secretary, 1999)
Jake Nevin (Villanova trainer, 1985)
Hank Nichols (Officiating, 2004)
Harvey Pollack (Statistician, 1995)
John Rossiter (Original Big 5 Business Manager, 1975)
Jack Scheuer (Associated Press, 2002)
Charles Scott (Penn assistant athletic director, 1981)
Al Shrier (Temple sports information director, 1984)
Bob Vetrone (sports writer, broadcaster, publicist, 1988)

Entering the Big 5 Hall of Fame in 1973 were (from left) Stan Pawlak, Wali Jones, Guy Rodgers, Cliff Anderson and Larry Cannon.

ROBERT V. GEASEY TROPHY
(Big 5's Most Outstanding Player)

1955-56: Guy Rodgers (T)
1956-57: Guy Rodgers (T)
1957-58: Guy Rodgers (T)
1958-59: Joe Spratt (SJ)
1959-60: Bill Kennedy (T)
1960-61: Bruce Drysdale (T)
1961-62: Hubie White (V)
1962-63: Wali Jones (V), Jim Lynam (SJ)
1963-64: Steve Courtin (SJ), Wali Jones (V)
1964-65: Jim Washington (V)
1965-66: Bill Melchionni (V)
1966-67: Cliff Anderson (SJ)
1967-68: Johnny Jones (V)
1968-69: Ken Durrett (LS), Howard Porter (V)
1969-70: Ken Durrett (LS)
1970-71: Ken Durrett (LS)
1971-72: Corky Calhoun (P), Chris Ford (V)
1972-73: Tom Ingelsby (V)
1973-74: Ron Haigler (P)
1974-75: Ron Haigler (P)
1975-76: Charlie Wise (LS)
1976-77: Keven McDonald (P)
1977-78: Michael Brooks (LS)
1978-79: Tony Price (P), Rick Reed (T)
1979-80: Michael Brooks (LS)
1980-81: John Pinone (V)
1981-82: Jeffery Clark (SJ), John Pinone (V)
1982-83: John Pinone (V), Terence Stansbury (T)
1983-84: Ralph Lewis (LS)
1984-85: Ed Pinckney (V)
1985-86: Harold Pressley (V)
1986-87: Nate Blackwell (T)
1987-88: Lionel Simmons (LS)
1988-89: Lionel Simmons (LS)
1989-90: Lionel Simmons (LS)
1990-91: Mark Macon (T)
1991-92: Randy Woods (LS)
1992-93: Aaron McKie (T)
1993-94: Eddie Jones (T)
1994-95: Kerry Kittles (V)
1995-96: Kerry Kittles (V)
1996-97: Rashid Bey (SJ)
1997-98: Rashid Bey (SJ)
1998-99: Pepe Sanchez (T)
1999-00: Pepe Sanchez (T)
2000-01: Marvin O'Connor (SJ)
2001-02: Lynn Greer (T)
2002-03: Jameer Nelson (SJ)
2003-04: Jameer Nelson (SJ)
2004-05: Pat Carroll (SJ)

ALL-BIG 5 TEAMS

1955-56
Dick Censits (P)
Kurt Engelbert (SJ)
Mike Fallon (SJ)
Al Juliana (SJ)
Hal Lear (T)
Bill Lynch (SJ)
Fran O'Malley (LS)
Hal Reinfeld (T)
Guy Rodgers (T)
Jimmy Smith (V)
Joe Sturgis (P)

1956-57
Mel Brodsky (T)
Dick Censits (P)
Dan Dougherty (SJ)
Kurt Engelbert (SJ)
Tom Garberina (LS)
Al Griffith (V)
Alonzo Lewis (LS)
Jay Norman (T)
Ray Radziszewski (SJ)
Guy Rodgers (T)

1957-58
Tom Brennan (V)
Dick Censits (P)
Bob McNeill (SJ)
Jay Norman (T)
Guy Rodgers (T)

1958-59
Ralph Bantivoglio (LS)
Bill Kennedy (T)
Bob McNeill (SJ)
Joe Ryan (V)
George Schmidt (P)
Joe Spratt (SJ)

1959-60
Bob Alden (LS)
Joe Gallo (SJ)
Jim Huggard (V)
Bill Kennedy (T)
Bob McNeill (SJ)
Bob Mlkvy (P)
Hubie White (V)

1960-61
Bruce Drysdale (T)
Jim Huggard (V)
Bob McAteer (LS)
Bob Mlkvy (P)
Hubie White (V)

1961-62
Bruce Drysdale (T)
Wali Jones (V)
Bob McAteer (LS)
Hubie White (V)
Tom Wynne (SJ)

1962-63
Frank Corace (LS)
Wali Jones (V)
Jim Lynam (SJ)
Jim Washington (V)
John Wideman (P)
Tom Wynne (SJ)

1963-64
Frank Corace (LS)
Steve Courtin (SJ)
Wali Jones (V)
Jim Washington (V)
Jim Williams (T)

1964-65
Cliff Anderson (SJ)
Curt Fromal (LS)
Matt Guokas (SJ)
Bill Melchionni (V)
Jeff Neuman (P)
Jim Washington (V)

1965-66
Cliff Anderson (SJ)
Matt Guokas (SJ)
Hubie Marshall (LS)
Bill Melchionni (V)
Jeff Neuman (P)
Stan Pawlak (P)
Jim Williams (T)

1966-67
Cliff Anderson (SJ)
John Baum (T)
Clarence Brookins (T)
Larry Cannon (LS)
Johnny Jones (V)
Hubie Marshall (LS)

1967-68
John Baum (T)
Larry Cannon (LS)
Mike Hauer (SJ)
Johnny Jones (V)
Dan Kelly (SJ)

1968-69
John Baum (T)
Larry Cannon (LS)
Ken Durrett (LS)
Mike Hauer (SJ)
Johnny Jones (V)
Howard Porter (V)
Bernie Williams (LS)

1969-70
Corky Calhoun (P)
Ken Durrett (LS)
Mike Hauer (SJ)
Dan Kelly (SJ)
Howard Porter (V)

1970-71
Corky Calhoun (P)
Ken Durrett (LS)
Bobby Fields (LS)
Bob Morse (P)
Howard Porter (V)

1971-72
Mike Bantom (SJ)
Corky Calhoun (P)
Chris Ford (V)
Phil Hankinson (P)
Tom Ingelsby (V)
Ollie Johnson (T)
Bob Morse (P)

1972-73
Mike Bantom (SJ)
Jim Crawford (LS)
Phil Hankinson (P)
Tom Ingelsby (V)
Pat McFarland (SJ)

1973-74
Joe Bryant (LS)
Ron Haigler (P)
Mike Moody (SJ)
Jim O'Brien (SJ)
Bill Taylor (LS)

1974-75
Bob Bigelow (P)
Joe Bryant (LS)
Ron Haigler (P)
Bill Taylor (LS)
Charlie Wise (LS)

1975-76
Norman Black (SJ)
John Engles (P)
Keith Herron (V)
Keven McDonald (P)
Charlie Wise (LS)

1976-77
Norman Black (SJ)
Michael Brooks (LS)
Keith Herron (V)
Keven McDonald (P)
Marty Stahurski (T)

1977-78
Michael Brooks (LS)
Tim Claxton (T)
Keith Herron (V)
Keven McDonald (P)
Marty Stahurski (T)

1978-79
Alex Bradley (V)
Michael Brooks (LS)
Bruce Harrold (T)
Tony Price (P)
Rick Reed (T)
Tim Smith (P)

1979-80
Alex Bradley (V)
Michael Brooks (LS)
John Pinone (V)
James Salters (P)
Rory Sparrow (V)
Boo Williams (SJ)

1980-81
Stewart Granger (V)
Kevin Lynam (LS)
John Pinone (V)
Neal Robinson (T)
Bryan Warrick (SJ)

1981-82
Steve Black (LS)
Jeffery Clark (SJ)
Granger Hall (T)
John Pinone (V)
Bryan Warrick (SJ)

1982-83
Steve Black (LS)
Bob Lojewski (SJ)
Ed Pinckney (V)
John Pinone (V)
Terence Stansbury (T)

1983-84
Steve Black (LS)
Granger Hall (T)
Ralph Lewis (LS)
Maurice Martin (SJ)
Ed Pinckney (V)
Terence Stansbury (T)

1984-85
Granger Hall (T)
Ralph Lewis (LS)
Maurice Martin (SJ)
Dwayne McClain (V)
Ed Pinckney (V)

1985-86
Rodney Blake (SJ)
Chip Greenberg (LS)
Maurice Martin (SJ)
Tim Perry (T)
Harold Pressley (V)

1986-87
Nate Blackwell (T)
Rodney Blake (SJ)
Tim Legler (LS)
Tim Perry (T)
Lionel Simmons (LS)

1987-88
Rodney Blake (SJ)
Howard Evans (T)
Mark Macon (T)
Tim Perry (T)
Lionel Simmons (LS)

1988-89
Mark Macon (T)
Doug Overton (LS)
Lionel Simmons (LS)
Mike Vreeswyk (T)
Chris Walker (V)
Doug West (V)

1989-90
Donald Hodge (T)
Mark Macon (T)
Doug Overton (LS)
Lionel Simmons (LS)
Chris Walker (V)

1990-91
Bernard Blunt (SJ)
Mark Macon (T)
Lance Miller (V)
Doug Overton (LS)
Randy Woods (LS)

1991-92

Bernard Blunt (SJ)
Jack Hurd (LS)
Aaron McKie (T)
Lance Miller (V)
Randy Woods (LS)

1992-93

Jerome Allen (P)
Bernard Blunt (SJ)
Eddie Jones (T)
Matt Maloney (P)
Aaron McKie (T)

1993-94

Jerome Allen (P)
Eddie Jones (T)
Kerry Kittles (V)
Aaron McKie (T)
Carlin Warley (SJ)

1994-95

Jerome Allen (P)
Rick Brunson (T)
Kerry Kittles (V)
Matt Maloney (P)
Kareem Townes (LS)

1995-96

Ira Bowman (P)
Marc Jackson (T)
Kerry Kittles (V)
Jason Lawson (V)
Reggie Townsend (SJ)

1996-97

Rashid Bey (SJ)
Donnie Carr (LS)
Marc Jackson (T)
Jason Lawson (V)
Tim Thomas (V)
Alvin Williams (V)

1997-98

Lamont Barnes (T)
Rashid Bey (SJ)
Howard Brown (V)
Donnie Carr (LS)
Michael Jordan (P)
Pepe Sanchez (T)

1998-99

Lamont Barnes (T)
Donnie Carr (LS)
John Celestand (V)
Michael Jordan (P)
Pepe Sanchez (T)
K'Zell Wesson (LS)

1999-00

Malik Allen (V)
Donnie Carr (LS)
Michael Jordan (P)
Mark Karcher (T)
Marvin O'Connor (SJ)
Pepe Sanchez (T)

2000-01

Michael Bradley (V)
Rasual Butler (LS)
Lynn Greer (T)
Kevin Lyde (T)
Jameer Nelson (SJ)
Marvin O'Connor (SJ)

2001-02

Rasual Butler (LS)
Lynn Greer (T)
Jameer Nelson (SJ)
Marvin O'Connor (SJ)
Ugonna Onyekwe (P)
Ricky Wright (V)

2002-03

David Hawkins (T)
Gary Neal (LS)
Jameer Nelson (SJ)
Ugonna Onyekwe (P)
Delonte West (SJ)

2003-04

David Hawkins (T)
Jameer Nelson (SJ)
Allan Ray (V)
Steven Smith (LS)
Delonte West (SJ)

2004-05

Pat Carroll (SJ)
Mardy Collins (T)
Allan Ray (V)
Steven Smith (LS)
Curtis Sumpter (V)

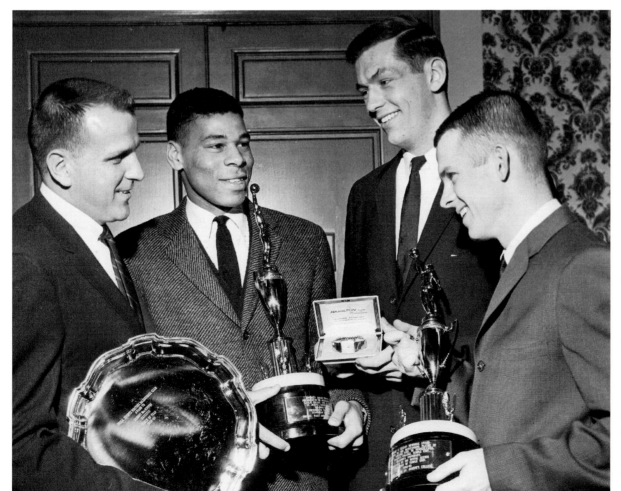

Wali Jones (second from left) and Jim Lynam (far right) shared the Geasey Award in 1963. Canisius' Bob MacKinnon (far left) was named Eastern Coach of the Year and Princeton's Bill Bradley was honored as the top visiting player.

Alex Bradley scored 1,634 points in four seasons at Villanova.

CAREER 1,000-POINT SCORERS

	Player		Yrs.	Seasons	G	Pts.	Avg.
1	Lionel Simmons	(L)	4	1986-90	131	3217	24.6
2	Michael Brooks	(L)	4	1976-80	114	2628	23.1
3	Mark Macon	(T)	4	1987-91	126	2609	20.7
4	**Tom Gola	(L)	4	1951-55	118	2461	20.9
5	Kerry Kittles	(V)	4	1992-96	122	2243	18.4
6	Keith Herron	(V)	4	1974-78	117	2170	18.5
7	Rasual Butler	(L)	4	1998-02	110	2125	19.3
8	Lynn Greer	(T)	5	1997-02	137	2099	15.3
9	**Bob Schafer	(V)	4	1951-55	111	2094	18.9
9	Jameer Nelson	(SJ)	4	2000-04	125	2094	16.8
11	David Hawkins	(T)	4	2000-04	127	2077	16.4
12	Donnie Carr	(L)	4	1996-00	105	2067	19.7
13	Doug West	(V)	4	1985-89	138	2037	14.8
14	Howard Porter	(V)	3	1968-71	89	2026	22.8
15	John Pinone	(V)	4	1979-83	126	2024	16.1
16	Steve Black	(L)	4	1981-85	102	2012	19.7
17	Bernard Blunt	(SJ)	5	1990-95	119	1985	16.7
18	Kareem Townes	(L)	3	1992-95	81	1925	23.8
19	Ed Pinckney	(V)	4	1981-85	129	1865	14.5
20	**Ernie Beck	(P)	3	1950-53	82	1827	22.3
21	Randy Woods	(L)	3	1989-92	88	1811	20.6
21	Terence Stansbury	(T)	4	1980-84	115	1811	15.7
23	Ralph Lewis	(L)	4	1981-85	116	1807	15.6
24	Gary Buchanan	(V)	4	1999-03	122	1799	14.8
25	Doug Overton	(L)	4	1987-91	123	1795	14.6
26	Marvin O'Connor	(V/SJ)	4	1997-02	110	1776	16.1
27	Guy Rodgers	(T)	3	1955-58	90	1767	19.6
28	Victor Thomas	(L)	4	1997-01	112	1765	15.8
29	**Larry Hennessy	(V)	3	1950-53	75	1737	23.2
30	Craig Amos	(SJ)	4	1988-92	114	1735	15.2
31	Ugonna Onyekwe	(P)	4	1999-03	118	1732	14.7
32	Tony Costner	(SJ)	4	1980-84	120	1729	14.4
33	Cliff Anderson	(SJ)	3	1964-67	84	1728	20.6
34	Norman Black	(SJ)	4	1975-79	104	1726	16.6
34	Maurice Martin	(SJ)	4	1982-86	114	1726	15.1
36	Nate Blackwell	(T)	4	1983-87	129	1708	13.2
37	Tim Legler	(L)	4	1984-88	121	1699	14.0
38	Jack Hurd	(L)	4	1988-92	124	1693	13.7
39	Mike Bantom	(SJ)	3	1970-73	84	1684	20.0
40	Bob Lojewski	(SJ)	4	1981-85	116	1682	14.5
41	Ken Durrett	(L)	3	1968-71	71	1679	23.6
41	Rodney Blake	(SJ)	4	1984-88	116	1679	14.5
43	Granger Hall	(T)	5	1980-85	115	1652	14.4
44	Aaron McKie	(T)	3	1991-94	92	1650	17.9
44	Mike Vreeswyk	(T)	4	1985-89	119	1650	13.9
46	**Paul Arizin	(V)	3	1947-50	82	1648	20.1
47	Keven McDonald	(P)	3	1975-78	79	1644	20.8
48	Alex Bradley	(V)	4	1977-81	111	1634	14.7
49	Tom Ingelsby	(V)	3	1970-73	87	1616	18.6
50	Bill Melchionni	(V)	3	1963-66	84	1612	19.2
51	Hubie White	(V)	3	1959-62	78	1608	20.6
52	Michael Jordan	(P)	4	1996-00	109	1604	14.7

a: Active for 2005-06 season.
Note: Includes those who played part of their career (*) or their entire career (**) before formation of Big 5 (1955-56).

CAREER 1,000-POINT SCORERS (Continued)

	Player		Yrs.	Seasons	G	Pts.	Avg.
53	Hubie Marshall	(L)	3	1964-67	74	1576	21.3
54	Harold Pressley	(V)	4	1982-86	135	1572	11.6
55	Johnny Jones	(V)	3	1966-69	80	1568	19.6
56	Jason Lawson	(V)	4	1993-97	131	1565	11.9
57	Bill Taylor	(L)	3	1972-75	82	1554	19.0
57	Boo Williams	(SJ)	4	1977-81	115	1554	13.5
59	Larry Herron	(V)	4	1973-77	104	1553	14.9
60	Ron Haigler	(P)	3	1972-75	83	1552	18.7
61	Pat McFarland	(SJ)	3	1970-73	84	1545	18.4
62	John Baum	(T)	3	1966-69	86	1544	18.0
62	Dwayne McClain	(V)	4	1981-85	125	1544	12.4
64	**Bill Mlkvy	(T)	3	1949-52	73	1539	21.1
65	Dan Kelly	(SJ)	3	1967-70	80	1524	19.1
66	Jerome Allen	(P)	4	1991-95	109	1518	13.9
67	Tom Greis	(V)	4	1986-90	134	1504	11.2
68	Stan Pawlak	(P)	3	1963-66	74	1501	20.3
69	Marty Stahurski	(T)	4	1974-78	109	1499	13.8
70	Mike Hauer	(SJ)	3	1967-70	78	1496	19.2
71	Rick Brunson	(T)	4	1991-95	124	1493	12.0
72	Carlin Warley	(SJ)	4	1991-95	114	1480	13.0
73	**Paul Senesky	(SJ)	3	1947-50	72	1472	20.4
73	*Hal Lear	(T)	3	1953-56	79	1472	18.6
75	Mik Kilgore	(T)	4	1988-92	124	1471	11.9
76	Eddie Jones	(T)	3	1991-94	92	1470	16.0
77	Bill Kennedy	(T)	3	1957-60	81	1468	18.1
77	Lance Miller	(V)	4	1989-93	121	1468	12.1
79	**Larry Foust	(L)	4	1946-50	103	1464	14.2
80	Howard Evans	(T)	4	1984-88	132	1459	11.1
81	Quincy Wadley	(T)	4	1997-01	128	1452	11.3
82	Bruce Drysdale	(T)	3	1959-62	81	1444	17.8
83	Bruce Lefkowitz	(P)	4	1983-87	104	1443	13.9
84	a-Allan Ray	(V)	3	2002-05	98	1434	14.6
85	Chris Ford	(V)	3	1969-72	91	1433	15.7
86	Larry Cannon	(L)	3	1966-69	75	1430	19.1
87	Wali Jones	(V)	3	1961-64	85	1428	16.8
88	Alvin Williams	(V)	4	1993-97	131	1423	10.9
89	Tim Claxton	(T)	4	1974-78	109	1418	13.0
90	Frank Corace	(L)	3	1961-64	73	1411	19.3
90	Lamont Barnes	(T)	4	1996-00	129	1411	10.9
92	Eric Eberz	(V)	4	1992-96	120	1397	11.6
93	Bob McNeill	(SJ)	3	1957-60	81	1393	17.2
94	Kenny Wilson	(V)	4	1985-89	137	1390	10.1
95	a-Steven Smith	(L)	3	2002-05	79	1389	17.6
96	Clarence Brookins	(T)	3	1965-68	83	1386	16.7
97	a-Mardy Collins	(T)	3	2002-05	93	1383	14.9
98	Larry Koretz	(L)	4	1983-87	120	1382	11.5
99	Bob Morse	(P)	3	1969-72	84	1381	16.4
100	Rap Curry	(SJ)	4	1990-94	107	1372	12.8
101	Paul Burke	(L)	4	1991-95	109	1368	12.6
101	Tim Perry	(T)	4	1984-88	130	1368	10.5
103	Jack Egan	(SJ)	3	1958-61	83	1363	16.4
104	Kurt Kanaskie	(L)	4	1976-80	105	1356	12.9

Eddie Jones scored 1,470 points in three seasons at Temple.

Chip Greenberg scored 1,227 points in four seasons at La Salle.

CAREER 1,000-POINT SCORERS (Continued)

	Player		Yrs.	Seasons	G	Pts.	Avg.
105	**Herb Lyon	(P)	4	1945-50	86	1333	15.5
106	Na'im Crenshaw	(SJ)	4	1998-02	111	1325	11.9
107	Pat Carroll	(SJ)	4	2001-05	110	1324	12.0
108	Tony Price	(P)	3	1976-79	86	1322	15.4
109	Tom Wynne	(SJ)	3	1960-63	85	1321	15.5
110	Mike Gizzi	(L)	4	1994-98	110	1319	12.0
111	Rashid Bey	(SJ)	4	1994-98	121	1316	10.9
112	Greg Woodard	(V)	4	1988-92	128	1312	10.3
113	Reggie Robinson	(V)	4	1974-78	119	1309	11.0
114	Stewart Granger	(V)	4	1979-83	125	1307	10.5
115	Jim Williams	(T)	3	1963-66	77	1306	17.0
116	Tyrone Pitts	(P)	4	1984-88	106	1301	12.3
117	*Joe Sturgis	(P)	3	1953-56	74	1292	17.5
118	a-Randy Foye	(V)	3	2002-05	98	1289	13.2
119	Bryan Warrick	(SJ)	4	1978-82	113	1273	11.3
120	Tom Sienkiewicz	(V)	4	1977-81	115	1271	11.1
121	Perry Bromwell	(P)	3	1984-87	80	1265	15.8
122	**Jack Devine	(V)	4	1951-55	113	1263	11.2
123	Rasheed Brokenborough	(T)	3	1996-99	96	1255	13.1
124	Matt Maloney	(P)	3	1992-95	83	1248	15.0
125	Charlie Wise	(L)	4	1972-76	97	1245	12.8
125	Barry Pierce	(P)	4	1990-94	107	1245	11.6
127	*Kurt Engelbert	(SJ)	3	1954-57	76	1243	16.4
127	**Norm Grekin	(L)	3	1950-53	88	1243	14.1
129	Phil Hankinson	(P)	3	1970-73	85	1236	14.5
130	Delonte West	(SJ)	3	2001-04	89	1235	13.9
131	Mo Connolly	(L)	4	1976-80	108	1232	11.4
132	Bernie Williams	(L)	3	1966-69	74	1230	16.6
133	Chip Greenberg	(L)	4	1982-86	110	1227	11.2
133	John Celestand	(V)	4	1995-99	124	1227	9.9
135	Dave Wohl	(P)	3	1968-71	81	1226	15.1
136	Hank Siemionkowski	(V)	3	1969-72	90	1224	13.6
137	Ricky Wright	(V)	4	1999-03	124	1221	9.8
138	Dick Censits	(P)	3	1955-58	76	1220	16.1
139	Mark Plansky	(V)	4	1984-88	134	1217	9.1
140	Jim Crawford	(L)	3	1971-73	77	1213	15.8
141	Mark Bass	(SJ)	4	1992-96	105	1205	11.5
142	**Fred Iehle	(L)	4	1949-53	94	1204	12.8
143	Alex Wesby	(T)	4	1999-03	122	1194	9.8
144	Bob Walters	(L)	4	1944-48	80	1193	14.9
145	Matt Langel	(P)	4	1996-00	108	1191	11.0
146	Kevin Lyde	(T)	4	1998-02	133	1188	8.9
147	Jeff Neuman	(P)	3	1963-66	74	1187	16.0
148	Jim Huggard	(V)	3	1958-61	75	1184	15.8
149	Rory Sparrow	(V)	4	1976-80	124	1183	9.5
150	Paul Romanczuk	(P)	4	1995-99	108	1179	10.9
151	Ed Coe	(T)	4	1981-86	120	1177	9.8
152	Tim Begley	(P)	4	2001-05	116	1165	10.0
153	Craig Conlin	(L)	4	1985-89	119	1159	9.7
154	Harold Jensen	(V)	4	1983-87	130	1155	8.9
155	Lonnie McFarlan	(SJ)	3	1980-83	86	1152	13.4
156	Jim Washington	(V)	3	1962-65	85	1146	13.5
156	Reggie Townsend	(SJ)	4	1992-96	111	1146	10.3

CAREER 1,000-POINT SCORERS (Continued)

	Player		Yrs.	Seasons	G	Pts.	Avg.
158	*Alonzo Lewis	(L)	3	1954-57	82	1137	13.9
159	Charles Rayne	(T)	4	1981-85	107	1131	10.6
159	Malik Allen	(V)	4	1996-00	125	1131	9.0
161	Billy Oakes	(SJ)	3	1963-66	84	1129	13.4
162	Donn Wilber	(L)	4	1973-77	90	1127	12.5
163	**Joe Lord	(V)	3	1941-47	71	1125	15.8
164	Koko Archibong	(P)	4	1999-03	116	1124	9.7
165	John Olive	(V)	4	1973-77	113	1122	9.9
165	Howard Brown	(V)	4	1995-99	127	1122	8.8
167	Joe Bryant	(L)	2	1973-75	54	1118	20.7
167	Joe Cromer	(T)	3	1966-69	85	1118	13.2
169	Paul Little	(P)	4	1979-83	104	1116	10.7
170	Jim McLoughlin	(T)	4	1979-84	104	1112	10.7
171	**Harry Silcox	(T)	4	1951-55	84	1111	13.2
172	Steve Bilsky	(P)	3	1968-71	80	1108	13.9
173	Tom Duff	(SJ)	3	1963-66	86	1103	12.8
174	Curtis Sumpter	(V)	3	2002-05	92	1095	11.9
175	Keith Parham	(T)	4	1977-81	98	1092	11.1
176	Romaine Haywood	(L)	3	1993-96	81	1083	13.4
177	Jeff Schiffner	(P)	4	2000-04	108	1081	10.0
178	Damian Reid	(SJ)	4	1998-02	122	1079	8.8
179	**Richard Heylmun	(P)	3	1951-54	79	1076	13.6
179	*Bill Lynch	(SJ)	4	1952-56	94	1076	11.4
181	Walt Montford	(T)	4	1975-79	107	1067	10.0
182	Corky Calhoun	(P)	3	1969-72	84	1066	12.7
183	Ollie Johnson	(T)	3	1969-72	83	1063	12.8
184	Steve Courtin	(SJ)	3	1961-64	82	1060	12.9
184	Albert Butts	(L)	3	1981-84	88	1060	12.0
186	Bob McAteer	(L)	3	1959-62	69	1056	15.3
187	Joe Gallo	(SJ)	3	1957-60	78	1053	13.5
188	Alton McCullough	(T)	4	1978-82	107	1051	9.8
189	Wayne Williams	(SJ)	5	1982-87	106	1048	9.9
190	Gary Neal	(L)	2	2002-04	57	1041	18.3
191	John Engles	(P)	3	1973-76	66	1038	15.7
192	**Barton Leach	(P)	3	1952-55	72	1033	14.3
193	Rick Reed	(T)	4	1975-79	110	1031	9.4
194	Mike Thomas	(SJ)	4	1974-78	99	1029	10.4
195	Jay Norman	(T)	3	1955-58	89	1024	11.5
195	Terrell Myers	(SJ)	4	1993-97	118	1024	8.7
197	Dmitri Domani	(SJ)	4	1993-97	121	1017	8.4
198	Bobby Fields	(L)	2	1969-71	52	1016	19.5
198	George Paull	(L)	3	1964-67	74	1016	13.7
200	Brooks Sales	(V)	4	1998-02	123	1015	8.3
201	*Jimmy Smith	(V)	3	1953-57	80	1014	12.7
202	Jim Lynam	(SJ)	3	1960-63	83	1012	12.2
203	Hassan Duncombe	(P)	3	1987-90	78	1009	12.9
204	Bill Phillips	(SJ)	3	1999-02	93	1007	10.8
205	Rich Tarr	(L)	4	1984-88	119	1004	8.4
206	Marc Jackson	(T)	2	1995-97	63	1001	15.9
206	Zane Major	(SJ)	4	1975-79	89	1001	11.2

St. Joe's Lonnie McFarlan averaged 13.4 points during his career.

INDIVIDUAL SCORING RECORDS

SINGLE-GAME LEADERS

Pts.	Player (School)	Date	Opponent
85	Paul Arizin (V)	Feb. 12, 1949	Naval Air Material Center
73	Bill Mlkvy (T)	March 3, 1951	Wilkes
52	Kareem Townes (LS)	Feb. 4, 1995	Loyola (Ill.)
51	Michael Brooks (LS)	Dec. 15, 1979	Brigham Young
48	Hal Lear (T)	March 23, 1956	Southern Methodist
47	Ernie Beck (P)	Dec. 30, 1952	Duke
47	Jack Egan (SJ)	Jan. 21, 1961	Gettysburg
47	Tony Costner (SJ)	Dec. 30, 1983	Alaska-Anchorage
47	Lynn Greer (T)	Dec. 3, 2001	Wisconsin
46	Bob Schafer (V)	Jan. 8, 1954	Baldwin-Wallace
46	Randy Woods (LS)	Dec. 31, 1990	Loyola Marymount
45	Joe Lord (V)	Feb. 5, 1947	Kings Point
45	Ernie Beck (P)	Feb. 6, 1952	Harvard
45	Larry Hennessy (V)	Feb. 14, 1953	Boston College
45	Ken Durrett (LS)	Jan. 16, 1971	Western Kentucky
45	Doug Overton (LS)	Dec. 31, 1990	Loyola Marymount
44	George Senesky (SJ)	Feb. 3, 1943	Rutgers
44	Larry Hennessy (V)	Feb. 4, 1953	Canisius
44	Bill Melchionni (V)	Feb. 16, 1966	St. Bonaventure
44	Hassan Duncombe (P)	Dec. 8, 1989	Navy
44	Kerry Kittles (V)	Feb. 28, 1995	Boston College
44	Rasual Butler (LS)	Feb. 23, 2002	Rhode Island
43	Bill Mlkvy (T)	Jan. 6, 1951	North Carolina
43	Bob Schafer (V)	Jan. 2, 1954	North Carolina St.
43	Lynn Greer (T)	Jan. 30, 2002	Fordham
42	Bob McAteer (LS)	Dec. 1, 1961	Millersville
42	Hubie Marshall (LS)	Dec. 1, 1965	Albright
42	Hubie Marshall (LS)	March 2, 1966	Louisville
42	Randy Woods (LS)	Nov. 29, 1991	California
42	Randy Woods (LS)	March 7, 1992	Fairfield
41	Paul Arizin (V)	Feb. 8, 1950	Seton Hall
41	Tom Gola (LS)	Jan. 6, 1954	Loyola (Md.)
41	Pat McFarland (SJ)	Feb. 9, 1972	Fairfield
41	Donnie Carr (LS)	Feb. 27, 1997	Fordham
41	David Hawkins (T)	March 3, 2004	Massachusetts
40	Ed Garrity (SJ)	Feb. 4, 1953	Rhode Island
40	Larry Hennessy (V)	March 4, 1953	Rider
40	Hal Lear (T)	March 16, 1956	Connecticut
40	Rich Moore (V)	March 3, 1964	Seton Hall
40	Bill Melchionni (V)	Dec. 11, 1965	Oregon St.
40	Hubie Marshall (LS)	Feb. 2, 1966	American
40	Ken Durrett (LS)	Jan. 28, 1969	St. Francis (Pa.)
40	Howard Porter (V)	March 2, 1970	Seton Hall
40	Ken Durrett (LS)	Dec. 9, 1970	Miami (Fla.)
40	Ken Durrett (LS)	Jan. 20, 1971	Niagara
40	Ken Durrett (LS)	Jan. 23, 1971	Lafayette
40	Steve Black (LS)	Feb. 26, 1983	Temple
40	Lionel Simmons (LS)	Feb. 10, 1990	Manhattan
40	Doug Overton (LS)	Jan. 31, 1991	Fairfield
40	Randy Woods (LS)	Feb. 9, 1992	Loyola (Md.)

SINGLE-SEASON LEADERS

Pts.	Player (School)	Season
908	Lionel Simmons (LS)	1988-89
847	Randy Woods (LS)	1991-92
847	Lionel Simmons (LS)	1989-90
836	Bob Schafer (V)	1953-54
801	Bill Melchionni (V)	1965-66
799	Howard Porter (V)	1970-71
792	Lionel Simmons (LS)	1987-88
750	Tom Gola (LS)	1954-55
747	Michael Brooks (LS)	1979-80
745	Hal Lear (T)	1955-56
735	Paul Arizon (V)	1949-50
731	Bill Mlkvy (T)	1950-51
719	Lynn Greer (T)	2001-02
714	Nate Blackwell (T)	1986-87
713	Terence Stansbury (T)	1982-83
709	David Hawkins (T)	2003-04
706	Marvin O'Connor (SJ)	2000-01
706	Kerry Kittles (V)	1994-95
703	Larry Hennessy (V)	1950-51
699	Mark Macon (T)	1987-88
699	Kareem Townes (LS)	1994-95
696	Michael Brooks (LS)	1977-78
690	Cliff Anderson (SJ)	1966-67
690	Tom Gola (LS)	1953-54
683	Mark Macon (T)	1990-91
680	Aaron McKie (T)	1992-93
679	Mark Macon (T)	1989-90
675	Lynn Greer (T)	2000-01
674	Hubie Marshall (LS)	1965-66
673	Ernie Beck (P)	1952-53
670	Rasual Butler (LS)	2001-02
670	Lionel Simmons (LS)	1986-87
659	Jameer Nelson (SJ)	2003-04

TEAM SCORING RECORDS

MOST POINTS, TEAM, GAME

LS: 133, vs. Loyola Marymount, Dec. 31, 1990
P: 115, vs. Muhlenberg, Dec. 1, 1969
SJ: 128, vs. Nevada, Dec. 15, 1971
T: 114, vs. Glassboro St., Dec. 17, 1951
V: 126, vs. Seton Hall, March 2, 1970

MOST POINTS, BOTH TEAMS, GAME

LS: 251 (133-118), vs. Loyola Marymount, Dec. 31, 1990
P: 202 (97-105), vs. Harvard, Feb. 10, 1990
SJ: 247 (127-120), vs. Utah, March 25, 1961
T: 197 (103-94), vs. Rhode Island, Jan. 6, 1983
V: 226 (99-127), vs. Canisius, Jan. 5, 1974

BIGGEST WIN

LS: 53 (94-41), vs. Youngstown St., Feb. 28, 1953
P: 51 (87-36), vs. Cornell, Feb. 1, 1974
     51 (92-41), vs. Swarthmore, Dec. 14, 1960
SJ: 65 (118-53), vs. Susquehanna, Dec. 14, 1966
T: 67 (114-47), vs. Glassboro St., Dec. 17, 1951
V: 92 (117-25), Naval Air Material Center, Feb. 12, 1949

WORST LOSS

LS: 42 (94-52), vs. CCNY, Dec. 15, 1945
P: 49 (98-49), vs. UCLA, Dec. 14, 1987
SJ: 44 (123-79), vs. Cincinnati, Dec. 11, 1959
T: 39 (68-29), vs. Kentucky, March 8, 1947
V: 47 (58-11), vs. Army, Feb. 12, 1922

INDIVIDUAL SINGLE-GAME RECORDS

FIELD GOALS MADE

Team	No.	Player	Date	Opponent
LS	24	Michael Brooks	Dec. 15, 1979	Brigham Young
P	20	Hassan Duncombe	Dec. 8, 1989	Navy
SJ	19	George Senesky	Feb. 3, 1943	Rutgers-Newark
T	32	Bill Mlkvy	March 3, 1951	Wilkes
V	35	Paul Arizin	Feb.12, 1949	Naval Air Material Center

THREE-PT. FIELD GOALS MADE

Team	No.	Player	Date	Opponent
LS	9	Kareem Townes	Feb. 4, 1995	Loyola (Ill.)
P	10	Matt Maloney	Feb. 4, 1995	Brown
SJ	9	Brian Leahy	Jan. 17, 1988	Duquesne
T	9	Rick Brunson	Feb. 26, 1995	George Washington
	9	Johnny Miller	March 16, 1995	Cincinnati
V	7	Doug West	Feb. 10, 1988	Temple
	7	Chris Walker	March 18, 1992	Virginia
	7	Eric Eberz	Feb. 18, 1995	Connecticut

FREE THROWS MADE

Team	No.	Player	Date	Opponent
LS	18	Lionel Simmons	Feb. 2, 1988	American
P	17	Ernie Beck	Feb. 6, 1952	Harvard
	17	Joe Sturgis	Dec. 17, 1954	Iowa
	17	Dick Censits	Feb. 22, 1956	Harvard
	17	Steve Bilsky	Feb. 8, 1969	Columbia
SJ	18	Bobby McNeil	Feb. 26, 1958	La Salle
T	18	Lynn Greer	Feb. 2, 2002	Saint Joseph's
V	21	Tom Sienkiewicz	Feb. 13, 1979	Penn

REBOUNDS

Team	No.	Player	Date	Opponent
LS	37	Tom Gola	Jan. 15, 1955	Lebanon Valley
P	32	Barton Leach	Feb. 18, 1955	Harvard
SJ	34	John Doogan	Feb. 18, 1953	West Chester
T	34	Fred Cohen	March 16, 1956	Connecticut
V	30	Howard Porter	Jan. 9, 1971	St. Peter's

ASSISTS

Team	No.	Player	Date	Opponent
LS	18	Doug Overton	Feb. 13, 1989	Holy Cross
P	13	Dave Wohl	Feb. 14, 1970	Brown
	13	Tim Begley	Jan. 18, 2005	Lafayette
SJ	14	Tom Haggerty	Feb. 21, 1976	Fairfield
	14	Rap Curry	Nov. 28, 1990	Drexel
T	20	Guy Rodgers	March 23, 1956	Southern Methodist
	20	Howard Evans	Feb. 10, 1988	Villanova
V	16	Jim Huggard	Dec. 4, 1959	Scranton
	16	Fran O'Hanlon	Feb. 24, 1970	Toledo

STEALS

Team	No.	Player	Date	Opponent
LS	8	Doug Overton	Feb. 3, 1989	Army
	8	Paul Burke	Jan. 29, 1994	Detroit
	8	Shawn Smith	Jan. 27, 1998	Virginia Tech
P	9	Ibrahim Jaaber	March 4, 2005	Dartmouth
SJ	10	Billy DeAngelis	Dec. 9, 1967	Bowling Green
T	11	Mark Macon	Jan. 29, 1989	Notre Dame
V	9	Gary Massey	Feb. 20, 1988	Providence

BLOCKED SHOTS

Team	No.	Player	Date	Opponent
LS	7	Lionel Simmons	Feb. 2, 1988	American
P	7	Tim Krug	Feb. 3, 1996	Columbia
SJ	12	Rodney Blake	Dec. 2, 1987	Cleveland St.
T	10	Duane Causwell	Dec. 26, 1988	Penn St.
	10	Duane Causwell	Jan. 19, 1989	Penn St.
V	10	Harold Pressley	Jan. 11, 1986	Providence

POINTS BY AN OPPONENT

Team	No.	Player	Date	Opponent
LS	52	Calvin Murphy	Dec. 16, 1967	Niagara
P	41	Paul Anderson	Feb. 26, 1983	Dartmouth
	41	Ralph James	Feb. 10, 1990	Harvard
SJ	54	Bo Kimble	Jan. 4, 1990	Loyola Marymount
T	40	Garg Spengler	Feb. 6, 1964	Muhlenberg
T	40	Steve Black	Feb. 26, 1983	LaSalle
V	49	Ron Shavlik	Jan. 29, 1955	North Carolina St.

INDIVIDUAL CAREER RECORDS

FIELD GOALS MADE

Team	No.	Player
LS	1244	Lionel Simmons
P	704	Ernie Beck
SJ	712	Norman Black
T	980	Mark Macon
V	918	Keith Herron

THREE-PT. FIELD GOALS MADE

Team	No.	Player
LS	308	Donnie Carr
P	253	Tim Begley
SJ	294	Pat Carroll
T	305	Lynn Greer
V	337	Gary Buchanan

FREE THROWS MADE

Team	No.	Player
LS	673	Lionel Simmons
P	469	Bruce Lefkowitz
SJ	532	Carlin Warley
T	482	Granger Hall
V	642	Bob Schafer

REBOUNDS

Team	No.	Player
LS	2201	Tom Gola
P	1557	Ernie Beck
SJ	1228	Cliff Anderson
T	1042	John Baum
V	1325	Howard Porter

ASSISTS

Team	No.	Player
LS	671	Doug Overton
P	505	Jerome Allen
SJ	713	Jameer Nelson
T	748	Howard Evans
V	627	Kenny Wilson

STEALS

Team	No.	Player
LS	277	Doug Overton
P	166	Jerome Allen
SJ	256	Jameer Nelson
T	365	Pepe Sanchez
V	277	Kerry Kittles

BLOCKED SHOTS

Team	No.	Player
LS	248	Lionel Simmons
P	195	Geoff Owens
SJ	419	Rodney Blake
T	392	Tim Perry
V	375	Jason Lawson

MORE GAMES

MORE NEWS

MORE PASSION

LIVE

Comcast SportsNet

SPORTS NITE

NEIL HARTMAN
LIACOURAS CENTER

comcast
SportsNet

COMCASTSPORTSNET.COM

Special Thanks to the 2005-06 Big 5 Sponsors

Title sponsor:
Freedom Credit Union

Supporting sponsors:

PECO Energy

Allstate Insurance

Philadelphia Insurance Companies

Janney Montgomery Scott

Cozen and O'Connor

Index